Just
Us Two

by
Rosalie Marsh

Best Wishes
Rosalie M

AuthorHouse™ UK Ltd.
500 Avebury Boulevard
Central Milton Keynes, MK9 2BE
www.authorhouse.co.uk
Phone: 08001974150

This book is a work of non-fiction. Unless otherwise noted, the author and the publisher make no explicit guarantees as to the accuracy of the information contained in this book and in some cases, names of people and places have been altered to protect their privacy.

© 2009 Rosalie Marsh. All rights reserved.

No part of this book may be reproduced, stored in a retrieval system, or transmitted by any means without the written permission of the author.

First published by AuthorHouse 2/9/2009

ISBN: 978-1-4389-2937-8 (e)
ISBN: 978-1-4389-2936-1 (sc)

Library of Congress Control Number: 2008912088

Printed in the United States of America
Bloomington, Indiana

This book is printed on acid-free paper.

Rosalie Marsh asserts her right to be identified as the author of this work.

The chapters on GoldWing travels have been previously published in an unedited form in the Gold Wing Owner's Club of Great Britain (GWOCGB) newsletter Wing Span for which the author retains the copyright.

To preserve confidentiality, the author has changed the names of characters both living and dead.

Photographs are the authors own.

To 'Ned'

Acknowledgements

With thanks to our friends in the Gold Wing Owner's Club of Great Britain in general and the North Wales Wings Region in particular for opening the door to ten happy Gold Wing years of discovery and adventure that we could only previously dream of—although not on a motorbike!

In order to check authenticity and accuracy of detail, the author has reviewed the videos made at the time and the author's husband 'Ned' has offered further recollections.

The Door Opens and a Passion is Kindled

"We have found it! We have found our lost youth!"

This story of the diverse travels of a born again biker and his 'chick' is an inspirational tale of discovery and adventure into the unknown by a pair of quiet, middle-aged, empty-nesters who had never crossed the water to tour abroad before. It is also a tale of courage and triumph over adversity as, following illness when it appeared that travelling days were over, they made mental and practical adaptations in order to continue to do what they could while they could and then they would not say *'if only ...'*

However this tale begins when, after a number of years bike-less, 'him up front' wanted something to tinker with and to get around on. At first he thought of a kit car and he spent the summer of 1997 dragging me around kit car shows. Eventually during a stay in Lourdes, France, in May 1998 he decided that he would like a little scooter and pulled me all over the town to admire different models. I of course wanted to travel through the countries we had flown over in the last ten years or so, in our search for sun and exploration of other lands.

'If we buy a scooter will you travel? Will you brave the ferry? Will you…? Can we…?'

With all these considerations settled we agreed that once back home we would visit local bike shops to look for a scooter. Scooter you ask. That is a rude word. The little scooter quickly became a large scooter. Touring France became a distinct possibility. On our return from France the large scooter idea fell through due to a lack of road handling and, to be truthful, he did look silly on it.

'There is a Honda Pan European 1100cc for sale,' Ned told me with a pleading look in his eyes. You know, that 'little boy lost look'. Need I say more and all at once we were emptying the coffers and buying a proper touring bike with lots of luggage space. This is an absolute requirement! Sacrifices only go so far. One bright Sunday morning there we stood, in our 'Sunday Best' as we had been to church, in the clothing department of the motorbike shop. We bumped into a colleague of mine who was startled to say the least to see me standing in high heels, smart skirt etc with a crash helmet on my head! I stomped around with heavy jacket and trousers and wondered what I had got myself into. Ned was full of beaming smiles and satisfaction. Another biker was 'born again'.

It had long been a dream of mine to visit Ireland and, hopefully, hear about Grandma and Granddad. To see where they came from would have been enough. Having decided to postpone our October holiday until Christmas just for once, a break in August seemed a necessity. It is strange how events seemed to take over as if someone was guiding us along a path. In the summer of 1998, having purchased our touring bike and, as I said not having toured abroad before, we thought we would test the water with a trip to Ireland before yours truly got carried away with planning to conquer the world. A dream would become a reality. This really was a journey into the unknown and a huge step forward for us but at least the language would be the same and you drive on the same side of the road as the U.K. so we would not have those things to contend with. As we planned our journey, we commented that we felt like "the owl and the pussy cat" of the poem, with only each other to comfort us if things got difficult as we travelled to this strange land. So, with quivering breaths and full of excitement we booked the ferry and I implored Mum to remember all she could and write it down. We bought maps, did our homework, booked hotels etc. And then fate took a hand ...

A Journey into Wing World

"The Owl and the Pussycat went to sea in a beautiful pea green boat. They took some honey and plenty of money wrapped up in a five pound note."
(Edward Lear 1867)

Rosie stood transfixed. She had wandered into the showroom out of the way, while Ned looked at the display of Kit Car models. His invitation followed on from earlier interest in them and, there it was ... the most beautiful creation you could hope to see. It sat majestically in all its glory, all gleaming black and chrome. It was huge with deeply padded leather seats, controls, and knobs worthy of an aeroplane cockpit. It waited patiently on its podium just waiting for them to fall in love with it. Ned came to see where she was.

'What is it?' Rosie asked in wonder.

'It is a GoldWing,' Ned replied and proceeded to point out all its features to this ignoramus. It was a gleaming brand new Honda Gold Wing 1500cc touring motorbike, complete with King and Queen Seats and, more importantly, bags of space for luggage with tailored bags in the panniers and trunk. They had reduced the price for a cash sale and although a bargain it was still more than they had.

'That is what we need if we are going to tour,' Rosie said.

Ned looked at her and, turning on his heel, walked outside. He thought he was hearing things. Dreams do sometimes come true but not usually packaged in the shape of the ultimate touring machine which they saw before them. Rosie continued to examine this beautiful beast—in particular the luggage space and comfortable passenger seat.

Ned came back and Rosie climbed onto the 'Queen Seat', the passenger seat, while Ned adjusted the passenger footrests so that Rosie's legs were comfortable. This was a defining moment. No more hanging on for dear life as they zoomed along the road. She would be comfortable! Ned continued to point out that the bike had reverse gear to make this heavy machine easier to manoeuvre, a radio so that they could listen to music as they travelled, a cruise control switch which could be set to a comfortable speed so that Ned could take his hand off the accelerator, an intercom system so that they could talk to each other as they rode along and crash bars at each side so that if they did fall over they could just climb out. It all seemed too good to be true.

'We could trade in the Pan European and get a mortgage on the rest!' Rosie said.

Bear in mind dear reader that they had only purchased the Honda Pan European motorbike two months previously and the top box only one week ago. *Where they mad or what?*

Ned could not believe that Rosie was serious and he needed no second bidding.

'You had better get signed up then,' he said.

Throwing all caution to the winds they took the plunge and did a deal. Ned thought he had died and gone to heaven!

On reflection—window-shopping on a Sunday is a mistake; a dealers dream but a mistake for us. It was a Sunday. We bought our life-changing bungalow on a Sunday and a few years hence would buy a new car on while out on a Sunday stroll.

However, back in the present there was some very quick work in our administration department, i.e. me, in order to get all the insurance and vehicle documents through and changes to ferry bookings made as we were due to leave for Ireland at the end of the following week on the Pan European. We had some panic as the current insurer would not go above £10k. Eventually, in desperation and not knowing of other Gold Wing Insurers at that time, we successfully went through Honda Insurance and the collection time with the motorbike shop was agreed. On our way home from work the following Friday, full of excitement at this journey into the unknown and with the cheque safely stored away, we both became stuck in traffic on the by-pass road around Chester.

I desperately tried to phone Ned but there was no answer from home. He was also stuck in the traffic. A hay wagon had gone on fire on the one of the slip roads. Ned had just gone past the exit for a slip road. It was four miles distance to the next one, which he wanted and he was just up in front of me. Eventually we arrived home and, in a panic contacted the dealer, in case he thought that we were not coming, to make fresh arrangements to travel up the coast the following morning on the Pan European. The deal done and full of excitement and trepidation we sat on our big beast. It had been many years since either of us had sat on a motorbike. I put my foot on the footrest while Ned held the bike steady and with a quick 'up and over' I was on. I adjusted the footrest and settled myself comfortable while Ned listened to a few last minute instructions from the dealer. Carefully, very carefully, Ned negotiated the turning to get out of the premises and, exhorting me to keep still and lean when he did, we slowly climbed the steep uphill bend onto the main road. We arrived home, after our virgin voyage along the coast road, on our big motorised horse without mishap. All was well, in the nick of time and we were all set for the journey to Holyhead the following weekend although Ned all at once realised what a daunting prospect the following week would be, by going to an unknown country on such a big bike.

Now, as I have said, the Gold Wing has ample luggage space with tailor made bags for the side panniers and the trunk. As I am the original 'just in case' type of packer, there were many deliberations and sacrifices made in the choice of clothes I could pack. Eventually we were to become more expert in this but this was now. I mean – how do you know what you are going to want to wear days ahead? Although I had to sacrifice hair, I refused to sacrifice glamour completely. Togged up like a spaceman in protective clothing, helmet, boots and with helmet intercom plugged in, we arrived at Holyhead after an early morning start along the North Wales Coast and through Anglesey to the Holyhead ferry, and were astounded to see a lone biker with a very, very small package on his tank. It was his luggage for a week. We would not want to be standing close on the way back!

Our journey of discovery across the water.

We really felt like 'the owl and the pussycat' as we set off into the unknown across the water, with only our trust in each other, emergency telephone numbers and our 'money' not, I hasten to say *"wrapped up in a five pound note"*. The ferry itself was an experience. I watched with ever-growing excitement as it came into view and disgorged its passengers, cars and Lorries. I had never seen a ferry before let alone loaded a vehicle onto one and was amazed at how big it was with huge funnels which sounded a greeting as it glided into harbour. Following instructions we rode up the ramp into the allotted space under the stairs of the deck above. Deck hands pointed Ned to some straps hanging up at the side to strap the bike down. They were well-used (i.e. dirty) and Ned said that if he had known he would have brought his own. He put his gloves underneath them to keep the seat clean and undamaged. With his baby safe, we made our way to the lounge. Ned, being a bad traveller was content to sit quietly and not move. I, on the other hand, was full of excitement and like a child in a sweetie shop as I explored the duty free shop and all corners of the boat. I loved to stand at the stern and watch the foaming water surging at the back of the boat as we powered ahead.

The crossing to Ireland was smooth. As we neared land, we were very excited as land appeared on the horizon. This was a dream come true. I had heard many tales from Grandma when I was a little girl and pleaded with her to speak a few words of Gaelic. I had tried to visualize what her Ireland was like. All I could imagine was that it would be very, very, green. (All the rain of course, but that did not enter my thoughts then; all I could think of was the romance and the mystery of her story). Through the mist, land appeared on the horizon. The lighthouse offshore came into view and, joy, oh joy, the misty shapes on the horizon came closer and closer and gradually loomed up to reveal themselves as—Ireland.

On disembarking, there was just a little excitement and consternation when we dropped the bike as Ned manoeuvred our steed the right way round. It was difficult as all bikes have to park under the stairwell and space was limited. The landing though was soft and there were many willing hands to pick us up after I had crawled out from under the crash bars, which are one of the beauties of a Gold Wing if the bike falls over. No harm done.

On leaving Dun Laoghaire we journeyed west. The landscape was green but oh so flat. The land was poor and scrubby and I wondered how on earth anyone could make a living. Surprisingly all the houses dotted here and there were new and modern. Very stylish they were too. Where has the money come from? This country was not the poor Ireland I had expected. After an early start in North Wales we were ready for lunch and stopped at a pub in a little village by a river. Suspicious eyes looked at us. Was it because we were strangers, or was the landlord expecting trouble from these bikers. We quickly finished our lunch and rode west. As we neared the west, the landscape changed and mountains came into view. After an overnight stop in Longford we journeyed on and rode into Westport, which is such a pretty town. One of the 'planned towns'. The following morning after a good night's sleep—fuelled by an excellent meal and wine at the Urchin Restaurant—we headed for Ballycroy on the far west coast.

The journey took us through Newport and over the river on to the Mulrany/Achill road. The mountains were nearer now and the coastline more rugged. The sun shone for us; it was a beautiful Irish morning. Through Mulrany, the road skirted the bay. The Atlantic had broken the land and it was as if fingers spread into the sea, curling gently as the water lapped the shore. Sheep and lambs were dotted along the road. 'Lamb chops for dinner!' But … look … look …the sheep are paddling and sunbathing on the mounds of land in the water, getting their feet wet. Would you believe it! I felt very close to Grandma at this point and very emotional. We passed a signpost for Claggan where Mum's cousin came from, but we will go on to Ballycroy. I took deep breaths as I realised with excitement that we were nearly at the end of our quest.

Our starting point was the church where Grandma and Granddad were married. We were to learn later of the romance surrounding this but, for now, we were only happy to find the family connection and maybe someone who could tell us where Martha lived. Martha is Mum's first cousin and they had lost touch after many years of writing. As our temperamental camcorder battery failed us yet again, from now on we had to rely on photographs—sorry Mum! There were many pointers to my family. In the churchyard was a tree and a plaque planted for one of Mum's Coffey relative's 100th birthday. Look! …a Moran donated a window here! …take a photo! All the benches had a family name and village; Coffey, Moran, and Cafferty!   Knockmoyleen—it does exist! Take a photo for Mum. Oh … Shranamanragh! Claggan! Take a photo of the altar also. A feeling of awe, that Grandma and Granddad had stood here to be married. The church was much bigger than I had imagined.

Coming out of the church, we took a walk down the road and I insisted that the Post Office was the best place to start. I stopped in my tracks as we tentatively entered what I can only describe as a whitewashed hut. A tiny lady peered at us suspiciously from behind the grille on the wooden counter. Surely the Post Lady was a relative. She was a 'dead ringer' for Auntie Sally! Taking a deep breath I enquired about my family who used to live here and a lady called Martha. I supplied her married name.

'Yes, that's right.'

Holding my breath, I asked: 'Is she still alive?'

'Indeed she is' was the reply, 'and has all her faculties and is very sprightly.'

'Ohhhhh,' I said as I let out my trembling breath. Our quest was nearly over. I could hardly believe it.

'Where can I find her in Claggan?' I asked.

Postie was very suspicious and guarded as she held on to the secrets of the hills.

'And what is Martha to you?' she asked.

I sensed that she threw up a protective shield. I braved the hostile look and, with rising excitement bravely ploughed on. Postie mellowed on hearing the connection and opened up as she agreed the levels of kinship. She said that Martha still dressed very smartly as she went to church.

'My mother also; she still wears high heels and fine stockings,' I gabbled on.

'Her daughter is just a step down the road. But you will need to hurry as she will be going to the Fleath' (i.e. a fair) in Ballina this weekend.' Postie encouraged us.

First, though, I wanted to buy a postcard to send to Mum. The shop next door would have one. This shop was a typical Irish one. The counter went right along into the pub next door as, in truth it was all one building. I insisted on a Ballycroy stamp and posted the card myself in the wall of the whitewashed building which was little more than a shack really. It would have a Ballycroy postmark for Mum. We used the last of the film on Postie standing against the Gaelic Post Office sign.

Off we roared on our Gold Wing following directions; left, right at the fork and past the two-storey derelict. She did not mention the cows in the lane. This lane was in reality just a cart track with ruts either side of the grass in the middle. This took some concentration on Ned's part to keep the bike upright. *(No matter how experienced a bike rider you are, you really do need to 'learn' how to ride a Gold Wing and we had only had it for one week. Yes, we are mad!)* We stopped to weigh up the situation. Oh, relief, a red van was coming the other way. The young man, a farmhand (as we thought), was laughing and waved as he moved the cows and calves (I never could walk past the cows on my other Granddad's farm in Lancashire). We took a deep breath and rode through the herd. In truth, only a little herd but cause for wariness nonetheless. It is bad enough riding a car through cows and *they* are not noted for their speed, only their bulk. Sheep are bad enough but cows! We safely negotiated a route, with liquid warm brown eyes quietly watching us. The lane is rough but better taken by a motorbike. We soon found Water's Edge—an apt name.

Knockmoyleen.
Unexpectedly, pieces of the puzzle fell into place when we found Bridie in Knockmoyleen. A man opened the door before we reached it. It was as if we were expected. Was it the bush telegraph from the Post Office? I stumbled over explanations. A tall lady came through a door at the bottom of the hall, standing with hands clasped. (On reflection later, I recollect that I stand like that at times of uncertainty and as I write this I realise that my sister does also). I break off explanations and blurt out that I think we are second cousins. Realisation came over her face and we shook hands and embraced. Bridie drew us into the kitchen. It was like being back in Grandma's as the kettle went on and plates and food appeared; ham, tomatoes and scone. Protestations were useless. They thought we had dropped out of heaven.

Family connections.

Pulling out my hastily scribbled family tree, Bridie and I compared notes. Conscious that we had disrupted her day, we did not want to linger. Pushing our protestations to one side, Bridie made telephone calls to family and started to fill in the gaps, well, some of them. Martha had more children that we thought. Bridie and I placed names on the roughly drawn family tree. I filled in gaps on our side and memories came back. Bridie did not know that Grandma had lost four children—yet she remained the most patient person I ever knew.

'Of course, your Grandma and Granddad eloped you know!' said Bridie.

'Did they?'

'Well, married in secret. As Patrick had no land coming to him, her parents did not want her to marry him. She was good looking and they thought she could do better.'

I told Bridie that Granddad always said—with a loving smile on his face—that "Grandma was the most beautiful girl in Leigh" and that even before she died she was beautiful. She had no lines and her hair was still blonde at the front. Granddad died two years to the day and at the same time of day, five or ten past four in the afternoon. (Strangely our eldest daughter was born at five past four in the afternoon and our second one at five past four in the morning. Nature has many unspoken answers.)

Bridie went on with her story of the great romance. 'The two families never fell out over the marriage. They also thought that Grandma was too young. They thought a bit more maturity was better before marriage.' Of course Granddad was five years older.

The young man we had seen earlier in the red van came in. It was Francis, Bridie's son and my second cousin once removed. Introductions followed. Ned said later that the family had sent Francis to direct us to the house. The bush telegraph had certainly been busy! We were though, not the relations half expected but a complete surprise. We had literally 'dropped in'. Mum had always said that Auntie Sally had been born on an island off the west coast.

'Where is Knockmoyleen?' I asked.

'No! Not an island but near an island, Achill Island. *This* is Knockmoyleen! She was born here.' Bridie replied emphatically.

Just Us Two

I explained that after Grandma went to Newcastle in England and the baby died, they came back to Ireland and Auntie Sally was born. They then went back to England and settled in Leigh, Lancashire. Two of Granddad's brothers followed and they settled in Llay—which is not far from where we live—in North Wales and they married two sisters. Neither of them had had children. Uncle Thomas is buried in Wrexham Cemetery and Uncle John moved to Lancashire. When Mum was about fourteen years old she used to visit for a holiday and walked the four miles to Wrexham Cathedral. She never dreamed that one day she would live in Wrexham. (They moved to Wales two years after us, to Wrexham and seven years ago we moved from the country into the town half a mile from Mum).

The old house.

Bridie decided to take us to the old house and show us around. I protested about her day.

'Ach—I've put it off!'

We were concerned but Bridie was adamant. There was some affinity here. We could both think on our feet. Leaving our Gold Wing we followed her to her car. The old house was still there, facing out to the sea down below. Although roofless the gable end was still intact. Looking around we could see for miles and miles across the sea into the distance and across to America. Oh, how could Grandma have borne to leave this land, this beautiful part of paradise where the Atlantic Sea lapped gently by the shoreline. The sunshine and breeze mingled. It was idyllic. Of course it would have been hard in Grandma's time. Bridie explained how the rooms would have been.

'That was Patrick and Elizabeth's room. This was the big kitchen and my Granddad had his bed in the corner. I was with my Granddad as I grew up. The far room was the best room. It was quite nice. This was the garden. Elizabeth used to keep it up and there were competitions.'

'Oh, how could she bear to leave this for Baker Street?' I cried to myself. 'No garden, just a back yard.'

(Years afterwards, Auntie Sally dug up some flags in the yard and planted roses. Grandma would have liked that). I said that it must have been an awful journey across Ireland.

'Well, they would have got the train.'

I lamented that I had not brought my little pot for the 'sod' which I had promised Mum.

'Take a stone from the house. A lot went off America.'

Ned stepped in and chose one from 'Patrick and Elizabeth's room. *(Mum's emotions overcame her when I later gave it to her and she could not speak)*. After a last look across the sun-washed Atlantic we went back to Bridie's car. Bridie was taking us to see Siobhan whose father was Granddad's brother. On the way we stopped at Shranamanragh Lodge.

'Are you still chasing the bumble bees around Shranamanragh Lodge?'

It was a beautiful clear day when we first saw Shranamanragh Lodge. Never in my wildest dreams had I ever thought to see the house where Grandma worked and, not only worked but that it was so close to Granddad's farm. It was a big house, painted white with curves and bays, it sat by the edge of the river at Shranamanragh Bridge with trees waving gently in the breeze. It was not a Doctor's house as we had thought, but a summerhouse.

'Possibly the Doctor came here. It was where the courting was done,' Bridie explained. (She went on to relate how an old lady used to tell her how Grandma ought to have married Joseph [Granddad's brother] but he wouldn't move in with her parents. Joseph went to New York and married the daughter of the Mayor). 'They along with another couple did their courting here. It was the courting house. After the wedding, the wedding party was here. An old lady who was at one time courting Joseph said that she had stolen a turkey from her mother for the wedding feast and cooked it. Her mother never knew. She thought that a fox had got it.' Bridie laughed as she spun the tale.

'There was no family at the wedding, parents etc. just the six of them. They were married on a Sunday evening in Ballycroy and had the wedding feast at the lodge. They later went to England but not before their parents had been told about the wedding.'

The school where my grandparents had learned their lessons stood on the corner by the lodge. Mum had told me that when she was small (five years old?), Grandma had stayed with Granddad when the rising river had cut her off and she couldn't get home. Mum had thought that this meant that *everyone* was cut off from the island. Bridie thought it more likely the weather was too bad and the river rose. Given that Granddad was five years older than Grandma, he must have looked out for her from an early age. *(I can just imagine Grandma as a little girl, standing with long blonde hair tumbling over her shoulders and with tears in her eyes as she realised that the water was rising and covering the road, pleading:*

'Patrick, help me. I can't get across the water!' and Granddad, tall and strong, shouting:

'Wait for me Elizabeth, I will look after you.')

It was truly, a love story. Bridie is the family historian and was with her grandfather at Knockmoyleen. Auntie Sally and Uncle Paul came to Ireland in 1939. Uncle Paul used to write to Bridie's father:

"Do you still chase the bumble bees around Shranamanragh Lodge?"

On this beautiful day full of profound emotional experiences, as I looked at this beautiful house, sleeping lazily in the sun by the river which ran under the road by the side, I could just imagine the scene. It is such a beautiful spot on the edge of the river with trees dipping down to take a drink to refresh themselves. Probably good fishing as well! On we went to see Siobhan down the road. Bridie had rung ahead to explain. Siobhan, Granddads niece, had tears in her eyes.

'After all these years,' she wept.

A peat fire crackled in the grate. Whiskies all round apart from Ned! A true Irish welcome. Martin—Siobhan's husband said that when the Irish say 'no' they mean 'ask me again and I will say yes'. When an Englishman says 'no' he means 'no'. I said that that proved I was Irish.

The English Connection.

Siobhan told us a little about Great Grandma Jennifer from Staffordshire (not Leicestershire as we thought).

'A true lady she was, a governess. She insisted on everything being just right and even ironed the babies' nappies. They all had to wear green ribbons. "You are Irish," she insisted.'

She apparently gave herself over to giving her children a true Irish heritage. This was certainly true about my Granddad as you would never have thought he had an English connection when he spoke of dear old Ireland. She showed us where the old house had been. Now demolished, the solid base is used to store peat. Siobhan was the daughter of one of Granddad's younger brothers. She explained:

'I had a brother who never married. Liked the dancing but never married. We (Siobhan and Martin) came back eventually to the Moran Farm. I am seventy-two years old.'

She had tears in her eyes as we left. When we got back to Water's Edge there was a crowd of young lads, who must have come across the fields, around the bike. They stood in awe and everyone thought that we were the rich relatives. Bush telegraph again!

To Achill and Claggan.

Bridie had rung her sister on Achill Sound. We spoke on the phone to Theresa and arranged to go after 3:00pm but first we must go to Claggan.

'It was all arranged,' she said

Theresa thought she had used to write to me (later, she thought it could have been my sister). Bridie said that Mum used to send parcels of Dandy and Beano and Girl comics that we had finished with. I remember that we used to have shamrock on St Patrick's Day and have it pinned to our coats to go to school. Bridie said that she used to pick it. It grows in the grass. It is strange how something so special to us in England is so ordinary in its native environment. Bridie insisted that next time we stay with her but; of course, we could not have arranged that for this visit as we did not know she existed. Bridie showed us wedding photos. The tilt of Martha's head was unmistakable and I exclaimed that I and our daughter have the same tilt on her wedding photos.

Following directions we went to Claggan. Remember that this part of Ireland is very remote with only the odd house dotted about the rolling landscape. As we turned off the very narrow road there was a very sharp, very steep right hand bend. I was nervous and climbed off the Gold Wing so that Ned could take her up himself, although he was confident that the Wing would handle it. It was a bit hairy! We stopped to ask if we had gone too far.

Just Us Two

'You will know if you have gone too far,' we were told, 'you will be in the sea.'

Eventually, when we could go no further as we really would have been in the sea, we came to a low white building. Martha's daughter-in-law came out to greet us. The farm was in another beautiful spot, on the edge of the sea with the land spilling down to sandy coves. Martha re-lived old memories and related how she had lost touch when Mum moved to Wales. She had written to Mum's old home one time but this proved a blank as the letter came back. Written on was the message 'no longer there'. Auntie Sally had moved out after Granddad had died and that was twenty-eight years ago. She was saddened to hear of Auntie Sally's death some years previously. She knew about Uncle Paul and talked about him; how Auntie Susie used to visit him. I know that Mum did so until he died and I related how Mum said that he used to look after the garden in the hospital and how he came to see us when he could. He always brought us sweets. (I remember once, when I was a little girl out walking with Mum as we made our way to my other Granddad's farm, that we saw this fine, tall, young man with jet black hair and that he was my uncle. What a tragedy that illness had cut him down in his prime). Martha told us that she had been ill. (Ned said afterwards, that she knew how serious it as even though Bridie thought that she didn't). Irish hospitality came to the fore again as there was ham etc. laid out. Refusing a sit down tea, we succumbed to tea and biscuits. After taking photos we set off to see Theresa.

'Such a short time,' Martha lamented forlornly, as if, having been given a gift we had snatched it away. She pointed out Achill Sound across the water. Following directions we went on to Achill Sound and Theresa.

'Ask at Moran's store for Thomas Ryan and he will direct you,' we were instructed.

Off we rode and reaching the main road turned right to Achill. Riding on we eventually came to a hive of activity and found the store. What a store! They sold everything. As I walked in, it was obvious that they were expecting me as I looked around and asked for Thomas. An assistant, with all the others looking on curiously, called Thomas whereupon he insisted on leaving his department and took us to his home. This was a lovely bungalow, again overlooking the sea. It was truly the most beautiful place on earth. Theresa came out to greet us and I thought she had a look of Grandma; Ned says that I could be taken for a sister of Bridie and Theresa. They examined my face closely as they remarked:

'Yes, she has the forehead,' and it was decided that I was a Coffey. Thus, they confirmed my lineage and claim to kinship.

After tea and pastries (again!), Thomas went back to the store. I had noticed that the wall display unit and corner unit were very similar to ours. Isn't it strange how people, miles apart, have the same taste not knowing that relatives have the same taste. Theresa chose it all. Both hers and mine are from Irish manufacturers. Theresa insisted that we stay for dinner, reassuring us that she would not go to any trouble. I said that we weren't dressed for visiting at dinner and my hair! Such a mess!

'You *are* dressed,' she said quietly but firmly. She is a very quiet and shy lady but very determined. Theresa suggested that we take a tour of the island and come back in an hour. If we were earlier it would be OK. We had a beautiful ride around Achill. The coastline was very dramatic and we spent so long that we were late for dinner. In fact we were so late they must have thought that we had gone home.

'How could Grandma and Granddad have borne to leave all this,' I asked myself, 'and go to live in a grimy Lancashire town?'

It explains why Granddad walked in the fields and lanes around my other Granddad's farm when he could, as he escaped from the darkness and confines of the Lancashire mines where he worked up to his waist in water for hours on end. It must have been purgatory but, as a small child you don't think of all that. It was a way of life for many.

Over dinner, we exchanged stories. Theresa and Thomas said that we had cousins in Newport. One lived on Newport Road near to where we were staying. Thomas asked the connection. Granddad's sister had married someone from possibly the same family. It had already transpired that we had relations in Australia and America. I think possibly the offspring of those who went to Newcastle-on-Tyne. (On a later visit a few years afterwards, more family details emerged, as Bridie had been in contact with a cousin in America). Theresa said that she had been named after Mum and she insisted that I ring Mum. When we got through, I asked Mum what she remembered. She spoke to

Theresa and was very surprised at the telephone call. I had a lot to tell Mum when we got home. Before leaving, Theresa showed us photos of her son's wedding.

Reflections.
We had said that we wanted to come back to Ballycroy to take photos but needed to buy a new camcorder battery. We forgot to take a photo of Theresa. She moved closer to me and we hugged our goodbyes. We could be friends …

For a couple of days we explored the area and strolled around Westport. I had always understood that Grandma and Granddad came from Westport and, in a way they did but further out. Westport was the big town and the easiest location to describe to 'the English' as the Irish community in Lancashire referred to us. The town of Westport is so pretty and a step back in time in some ways. The river flows through the centre of town dividing the main street. At each side, near the bridge, are steps which give access to the riverbank. We found the heraldry shop in one street and waited with baited breath as the origin of our family names were unearthed. I had taken details of the family tree and had scrolls made for Mum—one for Coffey and one for Moran—along with coasters. Dad later put these on the wall in the hall. We walked out of town along the road to Croagh Patrick and reflected that St. Patrick had climbed this mountain all those years ago when he landed in Ireland to convert the people.

Later we walked through the gardens, treading the woodland paths of Westport House and reflected that Grandma and Granddad would have been familiar with this area. One morning, following the Newport road, we started out for Ballycroy to take those missed photos. The clouds rolled over the mountains once again; the rain came down, at first in a steady downpour which then became heavier and heavier. It blinded us. It was like needles driving into us as we struggled to stay on the road and out of the sea. At Mulrany we pulled over as we were unable to see. We were at the point where the sheep had been paddling in the sea on our previous ride but the rain was so bad it was as if we had ridden through the sea. The workmen near the roadside had retreated to their van for shelter. Reluctantly, we retraced our disappointed steps back to Westport and the clouds followed us. After drying off in our

Bed and Breakfast accommodation in Westport we walked into town where we bought magazines and a notepad and retreated to the lounge of the Railway Hotel across from the river. It was time to reflect and, over coffee and later, lunch I began to write down the impressions and thoughts which I have shared with you. My head was whirling and as the words flowed I became very emotional. Ned was as moved as I was at the experience as Grandma and Granddad were really the only grandparents he knew and came with me often to visit them. Unfortunately, we were not able to re-visit Theresa and Bridie as we were booked on the ferry home and reluctantly left this lovely corner of Ireland.

In a way, history has repeated itself. We almost went off by ourselves to be married. We 'upped sticks' and went to a strange country—Wales—for a better life. With transport being what it was at the time, Ned's parents thought that we had more or less emigrated. Vision and stubbornness carry you through; that and being with the right person. The next step was to bring Mum to her beginnings. It was to be five years before this dream could be realised …

Onwards with Winging.

On our return home we set out on short rides to show our friends and relations our new purchase. As Ned pulled up in front of his brother's house he turned too quickly and promptly dropped the bike. Well, it is a big beast and once it goes over so far, the only thing to do is to let it. Picking it up is a work of art.

We went on to see old friends Marc and Mary in our hometown in Lancashire. They were out when we arrived in the evening and, on their return, could not work out whom the visitors were who had left all this biking gear in the hall. Mary sat on the floor and laughed like a drain.

'You are mad!' She kept saying as she laughingly shook her head at our folly. 'You are mad!'

I am sure she wondered if this was the quiet, shy girl she had grown up with.

Joining the Gold Wing Club.

Winter came and with it heated clothing for rides into the Welsh Mountains. Ned later wished he had not ridden in the winter due to the salt on the road which is not good for the bike. His road handling was improving all the time. In spite of many years of biking, the Wing sometimes needed a different technique. The intercom system on the helmets was brilliant as we could chat as we rode along. Ned wanted to know as much as possible about the bike along with information about touring and sent off for details about the Goldwing Owner's Club of Great Britain (GWOCGB). This was to change our lives.

Following this we went along to the North Wales Wings Region's monthly meeting in January 1999; or rather he dragged me kicking and screaming as I was daunted at the prospect of meeting a lot of stereotype bikers and bikes. This was a man's world and unknown territory. I would rather curl up with a book. I need not have worried as I was proved wrong. Gold Wingers are just that. Class and social barriers do not exist; the common cause is the Gold Wing. We received a very warm welcome and loads of advice about our plans for touring the continent. This opened the door to a ten-year experience which transcended all imaginings.

We had a lovely summer of Winging and joined in most of the Sunday runs visiting Rivington Barn in Lancashire which had been an old haunt of Ned's before he met yours truly; going to: Llfairpwll gwyngyllgogerychwyrndrobwllllantysiliogogogoch (or Llanfair P.G. as it is known), on the Isle of Anglesey which is Ynys Môn in Welsh; searching for ice cream on a cold day in Cheshire; riding in a convoy to Liverpool Airport with the winner of the Helicopter Ride. We also went on lots of rides on our own. At the Welsh Bike Show in Builth Wells—the grass tasted good—we almost went over the edge as we took the very difficult exit off the showground. I could see the drop in the ground ahead coming up to meet us and the only thing to do was to drop the bike.

'Hold on!' Ned shouted as he flung the Gold Wing to one side and we fell to the ground and slid along the grass, stopping just in time before going over the edge of the slope. Winded and shaken, I opened my eyes to see concerned faces above me. Ned checked that I was O.K. and then enlisted the help of onlookers to pick up this very big beast. We visited the International Bike Show in November and all in all we made lots of new friends. At the region's Annual General Meeting, members voted me in as Quartermaster and shortly afterwards Treasurer. These joint roles very soon became all consuming as Gold Wing activities took precedence and we embraced them wholeheartedly. In Gold Wing world nothing else seemed to exist and I fell in with it all. The Wingers soon made me realise that a Gold Wing was not just a bike—it was a passion. Do these Wingers realise what sacrifices and compromises their wife's and girlfriends make in the pursuit of togetherness, the biggest compromise being that of fashion and looking good? After all, once you have worn a helmet you can say good-bye to a nice hairstyle. A colleague remarked:

'Rosie, I can't imagine you wearing a helmet, not knowing how you feel about your hair.'

Of necessity, I had my hair, cut shorter and shorter and I found that a good cut soon fell back into place. 'A bikers cut' as someone remarked with a smile. This prim and proper, convent-educated Learning Consultant, had become, as another colleague said laughingly, 'a biker's chick'. In a trice I had overturned all previous perceptions of me.

One feature of the Gold Wing Club is the camping weekends which take place around the country in the summer. As we are not campers this is not the focus of our Winging, rather preferring to explore. In order that there was some social focus for those not Wing Dinging, our region set up a points system for those joining ride-outs to various venues. In 1999, the region awarded a shield to the winner and he named it the 'Way Worn Winger Award'. In 2000 Ned won this and proudly held the shield for twelve months plus a small one to keep. (He was to win it also in 2001 & 2002. Way Worn Winger became his nickname and I had a special pennant made for him to fly on the bike).We really had made some very big lifestyle changes. It was time to live a little.

Rosie outside Ballycroy Post Office

Rosie in Ballycroy Churchyard

Scenes on Achill Island, Co.Mayo, Ireland

Spreading our Wings

A gentle foray into the unknown

We had decided earlier in the year (1999) that we would venture into France to the Champagne region possibly visit the International Treffen in Luxembourg and maybe go onto Bruges in Belgium. I am lethal when it comes to maps and my imagination knows no bounds as I stick pins into places that look interesting. The big question was—how to go about the bookings. We had not toured abroad before, my schoolgirl French was limited and booking hotels was a daunting prospect at this stage. In addition we would not have the back up of a Holiday Rep as we were travelling independently. This was another ball game altogether. Looking in the Wing Span (the Club Newsletter) we followed up an advert for someone who would book everything for us and plan our route. This proved to be a good move as the directions were very detailed and gave us the confidence we needed and a point of contact for this, our very first foreign tour. It was 'just us two' …

As usual, we felt that the success of the trip was in the planning. After contacting the lady who would plan our route, we received lots of information, including the daunting prospect of finding that road numbers could change without warning. In addition, we had no idea what the road signs would look like etc. or even how we would manage the tolls. We agreed a route and price, with assurances that they would book everything for us and we looked forward to receiving a detailed itinerary so that we could pore over maps. We purchased Michelin

Green Guides of France and Belgium. We had found these invaluable when visiting Portugal and Italy in previous years, both for the town plans and information. We felt that we could not do without these. We also found a very handy pocket sized Michelin Atlas Routier of France which proved itself repeatedly. Forewarned is forearmed as they say.

Taking the motorways out of North Wales we eventually reached the Dartford Crossing. Stopping at the Thurrock Services before the bridge, I was surprised when, on coming out to wash my hands, two 'well-heeled' ladies appeared startled at the sight of me, and, abandoning their quest to dry their hands rushed out, finishing the job by using their hankies and whatever else they could find that was suitable. I had a little rueful laugh to myself. It is easy to stereotype people and there I was, a respectable wife, mother and businesswoman, being shunned by strangers. We were riding a machine which cost thousands of pounds, gear which was not cheap and I was being treated as if I was a potential threat. I told Ned when I met him in the car park, that I would love to go in dressed in biking gear and come out dressed in business suit and high heels carrying my briefcase. That would have made them think!

We set off and crossed the beautiful swooping bridge which spans the Thames Estuary on the east-west route. This was the Dartford Crossing and our first experience of travelling on such a high, long bridge on the bike. It was amazing. I had crossed it some months before when I was working and travelling in this area and wanted Ned to have the experience. The crossing to Calais was to be by Hovercraft which takes about thirty minutes. Ned was a bit nervous of this as he is not a good traveller but had resolved to tackle the journey. Following the signs we arrived at Dover in good time and, with seagulls screaming a welcome we watched in fascination as the Hovercraft floated in on its bed of air onto the flat land in front of us. What a revelation! The crew lined up, the front came down and the skirt deflated. Ned explained it all to me, even down to why there were fans on top. As vehicles disembarked we watched with baited breath as a car and caravan negotiated the dip where the ramp met the ground. We sized up the steep ramp and, recalling our experience on the Irish ferry, I decided that I would walk on to allow Ned to manoeuvre the heavily laden bike without worrying about me. Up and up he went and, with a sigh of relief, I saw that he was safe, so I followed on foot while he secured the bike. As Dover

Just Us Two

faded further and further into the distance we could see the White Cliffs grow smaller and smaller as we headed towards France and the start of our first journey into a foreign country by road. The channel was very busy with boats and ships of all shapes and sizes and we were surprised at the volume of traffic in what is really a very narrow strip of sea. The crossing was a bit bumpy and as we tried to make our drinks deposit themselves down our throats and not down our faces, we could not help but laugh. There was nothing to do but sit in the lounge and wait for Calais to come into view.

Disembarking, and with deep breaths, we followed the signposts and headed towards Boulogne. As this was our first time touring abroad, I wanted to 'see the countryside' and go on the coast road. We also had a lot to learn about French roads and customs. We were surprised how flat the land was until, that is, we worked out that it is on a similar level to the South of England as only the English Channel separated us. Surprisingly Ned found the flower covered roundabouts easy and riding on the opposite side of the road not a problem on the bike. We were also very relieved to see the road signs coloured white on green as in Britain. All in all he was relieved that he was coping with riding on the 'wrong' side of the road. We were going to be OK!

We had been booked in at a stud farm in Echinghen which is just outside Boulogne-Sur-Mer. Riding through the centre of Boulogne we followed the detailed directions and arrived in the village and our base for the night. The owners did not speak English and we (or I) had very little French. Monsieur came out to admire our baby and, using sign language, indicated that there was a bed for the night for our baby under the covered apple store in the yard. He moved implements and stores to once side to make room. There was no question in his mind as he was so impressed with what he beheld before him. We must not park outside in the open. It was a refreshing attitude and all without a word of English. 'Good parking' is a big consideration with a Gold Wing as a gradient can cause all sorts of problems including the bike falling over. Again we used sign language to find out if there was a good restaurant in the village, where we could have a good meal. After a wash and brush up, we went to explore and this restaurant was another experience. The Madame led us to the small garden area and a very, very, large, well-fed man wearing a blue and white striped apron gave us the menu. Somehow we managed to order and had a delicious meal at tables which had seen better days. We were in France! Savouring the real French experience! It was exciting! The following morning after a typical breakfast of coffee—very, very, strong coffee—rolls and preserve (in other words, bread and jam), we walked through the village which was still shrouded in the early morning mist to eye up the lie of the land and the road out. Strolling through the quiet country roads we drank in the peace and silence as we gazed around us. Behind a high wall was a churchyard and we saw the monument to the fallen soldiers of the World Wars. We could see the A16 in the distance as it stretched high into the clouds on its arches across the valley. Going through the ritual of packing bags in a set sequence we loaded the luggage into the Gold Wing. On saying our goodbyes to Madame and her sister, who had called to chat, they were very pleased that 'l'Anglais' had tried a bit of 'Francais'. With waves, Au revoir's and Merci's we saddled up to make our way to the Champagne region where we were to spend the next few nights. Following this, I kept a diary to record our impressions of our very first big touring holiday ever, not least on a Wing.

September 1st 1999.

Our route today had been planned to take us on more minor roads south of Echinghen to Hesdin. We travelled through countryside which stretched as far as the eye could see. It was more interesting now with leafy roads and glimpses of rivers. At Hesdin we stopped for coffee and a quick look at the village. This really was an adventure and all new to us. In addition we were relying completely on our own resources as it was 'just us two', the way we like it! Riding on, we followed direction to Desvres, travelling through a tunnel of trees at one point. Their shade from the ever-rising sun was welcome and we were enjoying ourselves and the freedom of biking. This more varied landscape was the home to long straight roads. How *big* France is! It must be seen to be believed. Through villages and towns we went and over the river to Desvres turning east to Reims. It was harvest time now and the huge hay bales were stacked in the fields.

Our lodging for the next few days was to be in a small chateau outside Fismes. Fismes is a pretty village to the west of Reims and we were on an arable farm. We had booked dinner for all three nights but the Madame, who was very distracted with a young baby and building work which was not going to plan, had not prepared for this.

'There is a very good restaurant in the hotel in the village,' she said. (She spoke broken English). 'My husband will take you in and just telephone when you are ready and he will come for you.'

We were grateful for this as, once we had showered, changed and prettied up, we—or at least I—had no wish to spoil a nice hairstyle by putting on a crash helmet and biking gear. Again, respect for our baby was duly shown as the Monsieur, when he came home, would not hear of us parking outside but instructed Ned to park up the bike in the barn. Ned thought that our Wing looked like a Dinky toy as the barn, made of stone, was so big. Climbing into a straw covered car later, Monsieur raced through the country lanes to Fismes. We had a lovely meal in the very French Restaurant although the menu which was entirely in French daunted us. It was no problem asking for 'Gin and Tonic and Coca Cola Light'. These are universal drinks. The food was another matter as I tried to remember the French for snails, rabbit and such like. Luckily, I had my phrase book and we managed to decipher enough to choose things we could eat.

Later, back in our room, we examined the touring brochures which our hosts had left for us and planned our itinerary for the following day. I cannot tell this story without mentioning the wonderful appointments in the room. The bathroom was en-suite but, as is common in France, only contained the bath/shower and washstand. The toilet was down the half landing, in the shower room. Therefore it was necessary to establish vacancy before making a dash for occupancy. We found the walls of the bedroom covered in the most beautiful yellow fabric. As Ned examined the construction, he explained that they had attached wooden frames to the walls and the fabric had been stretched across these frames to make a smooth surface. It all appeared to be in one piece; perhaps they had had it had woven specially. The drapes were of the same fabric. Outside the French windows was a huge square terrace/balcony with a stone balustrade which was actually the roof of one part of the house. The views across the Marne valley were amazing as rolling fields stretched into the distance. It was very quiet and peaceful with few buildings as far as they eye could see.

September 2nd, 1999.

After a good night's sleep and breakfast in the huge, elegantly furnished period dining room we collected our maps, togged up in riding gear over our shorts and T-shirts and set out for Reims. The sun was rising as we headed east. I was so excited as was Ned. This was a dream come true (one of many to be). We had never thought when we were first a struggling married couple that one day we would be able to see all the places we had learned about in school and beyond.

The car park was in Reims centre. We were a little surprised that the motorway had taken us into the centre of the city but, following signs we soon parked up. What a surprise to find that vehicles were actually welcome! 'Come in to our city,' the signs seemed to say. 'We will shade your bike from the hot midday sun while you explore the delights of our city,' the trees seemed to say. Another surprise was the addition of two hours onto the parking time which covered the lunch period where everything closes. What a bonus and how honest! In France, they do not charge for parking between 12 noon and 14:00pm when all France shuts down for lunch. Instead they add the time on to the chosen parking length. Divesting ourselves of our riding gear we quickly stored it in the panniers and, now wearing sandals, we had transformed ourselves into 'normal' tourists. Reims—here we come! Where shall we go first? I spied a Marks & Spencer's but Ned did not want to shop. Nothing changes there! We headed towards the Cathedral and were amazed to find that narrow streets ran around it and that buildings surrounded it. It was not as we expected and in truth, a little disappointment. Reims Cathedral is impressive to say the least; it is tall and narrow with a soaring ceiling and it was quite, quite bare of decoration. It was easy to imagine the French kings being crowned there in days gone by. There was a large chandelier hanging from the roof trusses and wall sconces which provided a great contrast. We found the outside to be very ornate with statues built into the design. Ned was busy with his camera and I was filming all I could.

The city itself is large with massive, ornate buildings and a large square. Using maps and a guide we headed towards the Mumm Champagne house. On the way, we stopped for lunch in a very French Restaurant. It was the type where locals eat; usually a good sign. It was lunchtime and busy but we found a table and using the phrase book managed to choose a good lunch as the menu was all in French. Leaving the restaurant we continued to follow the map through what appeared to be a poorer part of the city when, turning a corner, we found ourselves transported back in time. In awe, we strolled down a wide boulevard lined with large, white, period houses. Oh, can't you just imagine the carriages bowling down the street with the ladies decked out in all their fine dresses and parasols and all the men bewigged and powdered?

Approaching the Mumm Champagne House we found that it was a Chateau and very impressive. Posted on a board outside were the times of tours and we found that we were just in time for the next one. The display in a huge glass case in reception was of a great lump of chalk with a vine growing through and the roots sticking out. On reflection, it was easy to relate the area to the chalk downs of Southern England. We joined the tour and the guide took us in the lift down and down into the bowels of the earth. There were miles and miles and miles of tunnels, hewn out of the caves deep in the ground, where the champagne was stored; some of it very old, rare and precious. We saw the machines used in the making of champagne and had some excellent demonstrations and a lesson on the champagne making process. As usual, the tour ended with a visit to the shop where our guide offered us a tasting. Ned is not a wine lover but tried the Demi Sec (Green Label). This in itself was a surprise as we had thought that all champagne was Brut. After a couple of sips and the usual face pulling Ned passed his glass to me so that the delicious champagne was not wasted.

That night we had been promised dinner on the farm and, on our return saw an English car in the yard. It was a young couple on their way to the Italian Grand Prix. We all met in the salon for aperitifs before sitting down in the beautiful dining room to eat at the large table. These rooms had the same method of decoration as our bedroom. The rose coloured fabric adorning the walls had matching drapes at the long windows, with the furniture being of period style. The temperamental Madame had a small baby, lots of crisises and was in floods of tears. A friend in Paris had died. She was desolate but Monsieur saved the day and after champagne aperitifs in the salon, served a wonderful meal of fish.

September 3rd, 1999.

Today we had planned to tour the Champagne Route. This would take us through the vineyards and villages and we planned to visit some famous places. Travelling along roads amid the vineyards, with miles and miles of vines we soon came to Abbeville where Dom Perignon, who started the Champagne story, is buried. We had been surprised that the vines grew at the side of the road as we had expected all the vineyards to be behind closed walls. All vines have labels with the grape type and the champagne house for which they are destined. Moet & Chandon now privately own Abbeville Abbey but we were able to go into the church and visit Dom Perignon's tomb. The village is delightful; all green with flowers tumbling over high walls in the lanes. Some locals asked if we wanted to come into the cellars and taste the wine. We demurred as, still novices at touring, we were shy. It would be a different story a few years hence as we found our touring feet.

We travelled on to Epernay where we were disappointed in the town in that, it was quite unremarkable. It was just a typical French town and we had perhaps expected too much as we (or rather I) had a romantic view of the whole area. After all, it is the capital of the Champagne region. Continuing, we rode west through Condé en Brie (oh! the cheese) to Chateau Thierry. This is actually a town not a Chateau. Everywhere we journeyed today, this wonderful day of bright sunshine and promise of new experiences, we saw masses of blooms. If only the watering facilities were as enjoyable in this old town. Finding a café, I sent Ned off to reccae the toilets. He came back with a shake of his head. They were the 'two feet in the ground across a hole' variety and awash! Ughhh! Hang on—find somewhere else! This was easier said than done as hotels were few and far between. In addition, as we rode on, fuel was low.

'Where are the Petrol Stations?' we asked each other.

The intercom was coming very handy indeed as we discussed directions. We stopped in a village to ask a local, using sign language. From what I remember our petrol had to last out until we reached Fismes where thankfully, Ned was able to fill up on petrol. That night, we ate out in Fismes once again with the owner chauffeuring us there and back. As it was the second visit, the owner of this Logis de France Hotel greeted us like old friends. The following morning, Saturday as we prepared to leave we saw a wonderful sight. Floating over the Marne valley towards the house were many, many balloons of all colours. They had come from twenty kilometres away. It was totally unexpected and a wonderful end to our visit. As the balloons floated over our balcony and I stood outside on the balcony to watch, there were shouts of 'Bonjour!' as they floated over the house and away.

'Bonjour!' I returned excitedly. This was a lovely, unexpected end to our stay in this part of France.

We packed our luggage, said our 'Au revoir's' and 'Merci's' and set out for Luxemburg. Heading eastwards towards Reims we missed the turning for the motorway. Confusingly, if you want the motorway you head towards Reims Centre as it runs across the bottom of the city. Instead we headed away from the city (as we thought) and actually ended up right in the centre, on cobbles, in the Market Square. The main road out to follow now was the 'green' sign and not a 'blue' one as we wanted. We decided that, 'well it doesn't matter as long as we end up where we want to'. The road was a long one and very straight, as far as they eye could see and quite boring. Near the Luxemburg border at about noon, we stopped in a village for lunch. As I have noted before, the custom in France is for lunchtime to stop all activities for two hours and we found all the shops closed. It was like a ghost village. There was also no food! We travelled on and, stopping for petrol; we bought a welcome sandwich in the shop. As it was getting late by now in Luxemburg we abandoned our plans to visit the Gold Wing Treffen. Instead, we followed directions which took us through the city centre and headed for the Ibis hotel, shower and dinner. Although our 'trip' through Luxemburg was a short one it was interesting to get a brief taste of what it had to offer and convinced us that it would be worth a longer trip one day.

September 5th, 1999.

The following morning we headed into Belgium for Bruges. Our route took us through the Ardennes. The thick forests were very green and, again, the roads were long and straight stretching into the distance with miles and miles of motorway bounded by trees. As usual, I wanted to see and experience everything and so, with my usual plea and bright ideas of 'why don't we …?' we headed for Brussels. We had to stop and take stock as we were not sure of our route out of the city. I had with me the Green Michelin book and used the street map to follow the route and direct Ned. All this while I was filming of course! I saw a sign for the Notre Dame Cathedral so I urged Ned to 'go down there!' Oops!! We were on cobbles, across tramlines with a fully loaded bike and tight turns. Well done Ned! We followed the road through the underpass which took us out of the city (again, this is worth a longer visit) and onto the road to Bruges and our Ibis hotel. This hotel is situated in the old part of the city and again the streets were paved with cobbles. It was quite nerve-racking and challenging for Ned to negotiate them whilst following road signs and finding the hotel. I just kept quiet and held my breath. The hotel was part of an old convent, retaining some of the original walls but it was quite modern inside. We soon settled in, showered, changed and set off to do some gentle exploration and to get our bearings.

During our stay in Bruges, we sampled as much as we could of the culture, canals, shops, way of life and chocolate. The latter is a must as it is so famous! The shops were full of not only Belgian lace but also Bruges lace which is also famous. Belgian lace is very fine and delicately made but Bruges lace is even finer and has the 'Rose of Bruges' in the centre. They use the lace to make lifelike dressed dollies and all manner of other souvenirs such as serving tray and tabletop inserts under glass. Of particular temptation were the displays of sweets and chocolates in wonderful fruit shapes and colours.

Using our Michelin Green Guide, we continued our exploration into the central square. This is a large cobbled square surrounded by old buildings. Horse-drawn carriages vied for space with scooters and sports cars. We decided to climb the Bell Tower or Campanile and, as is my usual practice, I was wearing gold mules one of which I almost lost as we climbed on and on up the spiral staircase. As one fell off it dropped down the stairwell and a tourist retrieved it after we passed down a call for help. The effort of climbing and huffing and puffing up 350 steps was well worth it as the views are stupendous. The bells are very effective also when they ring out while you are standing at the side of them. Consequently, everyone claps their hands over their ears until the ringing stopped. Ned, as could be expected, was very interested in the engineering aspect of the bells and made a fascinated examination of the workings of the cogs and wheels while I admired the view which stretched for miles around.

Bruges is full of canals and waterways and a trip on a boat was a delightful way to while away the afternoon and must be experienced to be believed. The guide explained about all the buildings and the architecture and history of Bruges as the boat wended its way through the tree-shaded water which lapped at its sides in the stillness of the afternoon on these quiet waterways.

The language in Bruges, although very different is easy to work out. The town is delightful and at one point, as I had no spectacles on, I used the camcorder to examine the town map. This city where the main mode of transport is bicycle is delightful with modern shops. As is common on the continent, the shopkeepers wash the pavement every morning. Each day brought something new as we explored this charming city, ending our stay with a stroll around Minnewater Park and a reccae of the road out for the journey back to Calais, Dover and home. It was now time to tuck in our wings, rest in our nest and put the baby to bed.

On a Wing and a Prayer

"the birds soared lazily above in the cloudless blue sky. We soared below…"

As 'born again bikers' we had lots of plans to conquer the world. We set off on our second summer of Winging in May 2000.

Travels continued with our long planned journey through France to Lourdes in the Pyrénées. In addition, two club members organised a 'Drop Out' in Andorra and as this worked in well with our trip to Lourdes at the west end of the Pyrénées, we could not say no. *(A Drop Out is an informal gathering of Wingers and usually a bit more low key to the usual official Wing Ding events in the United Kingdom. Even so, they have to be well organised).* I had negotiated 'accommodation only' with the travel firm who organised the Lourdes pilgrimages and only had to book hotels en route. The main problem now was packing the trunk and panniers of the Gold Wing with enough, but not too many, clothes etc. As anyone who knows me well will realise, this would take some sacrifices. Normally, Ned has to order me to reduce the weight in a *suitcase*, so you can see the scale of the problem. All was well that ended well and we embarked on our first tunnel crossing.

Our only other experience of crossing the channel was by Hovercraft, and even a mildly choppy sea is not good news for a bad traveller. The Channel Tunnel was the answer. Folkestone Terminal was well organised. After passing the check-in point we settled ourselves in the terminal building where I was able to explore the shops. It was a bit nerve-racking keeping our eye on the departure board as it was all very unfamiliar, and we were not too sure when our call would come. In the end, I said that I thought that we should make a move as others who had booked in when we did had gone. We followed all the signs and passing through security went down the ramps into the designated lane. The arrangement for bikes is that they go on last. When called, we slowly went down all the ramps onto the platform and saw a big hole in the side of the train where the sides had opened. We rode on, parked up on the side stand and stayed with the bike. Thirty-five minutes later we were riding forward down the length of the train and onto French soil. The sky was clear; even the air smelt different to England. In great excitement we set off. Firstly, though Ned needed to give his baby a big drink so we stopped at the service station near the exit, filled her up and went inside for a drink for us. Even this was an experience. It had all been so easy, and we followed the signs which would take us down the west coast of France to Anger.

We stopped at Anger with time to explore a little. Our hotel was in a delightful spot in the centre of the city, by the side of the river which runs through the city. It was a delightful spot with the water glistening in the sunshine and people strolling by the riverside under the many trees which provided welcome shade. Ned soon found the secure parking around the corner and put his baby securely to bed while I checked in and did all the administration needed. After we had unloaded, showered and changed, we stretched our legs by strolling to the cathedral and climbing the many steps up to the entrance before wandering into the lively shopping area.

The following morning, our journey continued south via Bordeaux, keeping to the motorways in order to cover the miles within the planned time-scale. As we travelled on, the air became hotter and hotter and the rest areas at the side of the motorways were very welcome. We had booked a hotel just outside Biarritz (by the Airport for ease of location), but were undecided whether to go into the town to explore. However, as a nice Frenchman had tried to lift our pannier off with his bumper bar when on a roundabout outside Biarritz, we ended up at the Police Station in town the following morning to report the incident. (The local Gendarmerie, next door to the hotel had closed the previous evening and in any case, when they opened the following morning they were not interested and didn't speak English). The hotel receptionist was excellent in using the telephone for us to sort out this problem as there was very little English spoken in this part of the country. This is one good reason for using a recognised chain of hotels—as well as learning French! Thus we saw Biarritz in the end, which had been the original reason for going that route to our destination. It did not live up to expectations, and was more like a very grand but faded British seaside town. The Frenchman had insisted that it was our fault and had become very voluble when we showed him the damage. As soon as he saw that I was filming, he hastily got back in his car and drove off with his passenger. In the Police Station in Biarritz we played back the film I taken on the camcorder, for the Police Inspector who only spoke a little but welcome English. In the event this proved useful for our insurance company when we got back home, as the man had put in a claim against us!

Travelling along the foothills of the Pyrénées to Lourdes on an almost deserted road, we really did feel like pioneers; as if no one had gone before us. We had only our own resources to draw on. Petrol Stations were few and far between once when off the major roads. However, in France there is an excellent system of having areas made especially for a rest and with facilities for comfort stops. One of these consisted of a lone building set in an otherwise deserted piece of land. The architecture was very streamlined and attractive with the building having a roof in the shape of a cone. The facilities were very clean and one could only wonder at the organisation in place for their upkeep. The statue (or monument) by the parking area had a descriptive plaque which explained about historical facts of the area.

Riding on to Lourdes and passing a Gold Wing just outside the town, we arrived safely at our very modern hotel by the River Gave, meeting up with old friends from home for a few days. They had come in by aeroplane and coach and our Bishop had remarked on the co-incidence of the motorbike parked outside the hotel having a North Wales number plate. The Bishop was 'bowled over' to find that it belonged to two of his flock. He was delighted at our enterprise. Our former Parish Priest was astounded and delighted to see us again and could not get over how we had travelled to this remote area and little town in the foothills of the mountains, not only on our own but on a motorbike. Although we had travelled independently, we joined in with the planned programme of the Diocese as we had hoped to. We met up with another former Parish Priest and others and they all thought that we were wonderful in riding to Lourdes on a motorbike and could not get over our adventures, especially when we said that we were to go on to Andorra. They had all known us for many years and in their eyes, this did rather seem to be a complete departure for us and it was rather hard for them all to take in.

The Military from all over the world were back in town for their biennial pilgrimage and one night an American group set up their band in a street junction by the old bridge causing a traffic jam as all the crowds on their way back from the Domaine and Torchlight Procession to the bars, stopped to listen, singing and clapping along with the jazzy songs. Lourdes is a place of prayer, yes, but it is also a place of peace and enjoyment and in fact, the bars do not close until the last customer has gone but no matter what time that is, they are all opening up 7:30am the following morning. After all—business is business isn't it?

At the end of our stay, we loaded up and our group waved us off as we headed—just us two—along the foothills of the Pyrénées from Lourdes for an overnight stop in Carcassonne, before starting the second leg of our trip in Andorra to meet twenty-one Gold Wings, six racing bikes and three cars. This overnight stop bridged the gap between the two very different parts of the tour.

Carcassonne remains a walled medieval city with both inner and outer walls and towers intact. Inside, there is a thriving community in the original buildings. We had plenty of time to explore both the old and new town, after putting the bike in the secure parking under our Ibis hotel on the Square Gambetta. We had dinner in a small restaurant across the square which one of the Andorran trip organisers had recommended to us. This kind of help is invaluable as we find it real concern in a strange country to know if we are going to find a decent restaurant. We then went to draw out more cash. We were not sure if it would be Euros or English pounds as it was the first time we had used a French Cash Machine As there had been a bank strike, the cash machines had not been working and the hotel receptionist was relieved to hear that he could at last draw out some money. The maps provided in the Hotel Directory had allowed us to make a considered judgement to the feasibility of each hotel location *v* travelled route. Invaluable!

A testing time in Andorra.

From Carcassonne we travelled south through Foix, admiring the very pretty view of sunlight on the snow-capped mountains and fluffy clouds in the distance. They were so pretty. When planning this trip I had bought a regional map of Andorra which, being on a large scale showed a true picture of the terrain. I had got quite frightened and almost changed my mind about the safety of the trip when I saw the bends and the heights of the mountains. Ned had been very reassuring as he compared these to the mountain roads in North Wales which we take for granted. As we now admired these snow capped mountains, we did not realise that we would be riding through these passes and wondered how much higher we could go. Quite a lot, as we soon found out and we did not envy the mountain cyclists, which we overtook, their gruelling climb on the switchback roads which climbed to the clouds and beyond. The comfort of a Gold Wing is a much better option. I actually realised then, just why they were called mountain bikes! The mountains with their high majestic peaks glinting in the sunshine while white fluffy clouds floated by in a bright blue sky, closed in on us as we rode on and as we climbed higher and higher we went through the mist.

The Pas de la Casa is spectacular and we were to cross back and to throughout the week as it is the only way in and out of France. At six to seven thousand feet high, the journey often involves cloud travel (i.e. no can see!), with brilliant sunshine just around the corner. The Border Post between Andorra and France was in quite a desolate spot and at this point, in what seemed to be the top of the world. We could hardly see in front of us and wondered just what we had done and what would come next. With deep breaths we rode on through the cloud coming back into brilliant sunshine as we covered the Pass, arriving in Soldeau to find that one of the party organisers had ridden out on the road looking for arrivals. Oh, the relief!

'Look, we are nearly there', I shouted to Ned through the intercom.

We novices were the first! What a welcome sight and confirmation that we had made it and not got lost. Delightedly, the organisers escorted us on the last short lap of our journey and, first things first, through the car park to settle the Wing into the heated garage and take stock of our surroundings. Suffice to say that they were relieved that at least one of the party had arrived safely to this remote spot in the Pyrénées. It was such a long way from home and had been quite an undertaking. We took the view that 'nothing ventured, nothing gained'. Our four star hotel was excellent and we took advantage of a dip in the indoor pool and outdoor Jacuzzi hot tub, followed by a spot of sunbathing with mountains surrounding us. With a launderette across the road, to drop a bag of washing into, our packing sacrifices were not a problem. Our journey into the unknown so far had been one which had drawn on more inner resources than we knew we had as we pushed back our personal boundaries in this adventure.

There was a good mix of planned runs and time to explore at will. Andorra is beautiful, spectacular, and hot. The Andorrans from the local club made us very welcome and on the Sunday—the first day after arrival—some of them from the Goldwing Club of Andorra acted as guides and marshal's for the run-out through Encamp and Andorra-la-Vella (the main town), before escorting us up the mountains to Ordino and beyond. Beyond—being the operative word!

After an introductory meeting in the hotel they took us out on a day of contrasts, which introduced the delights of Andorra. The weather in what was by now the third week of May and in-between seasons was scorching hot. We visited a motorbike museum which had a very quaint early motorbike on display which looked nothing like the ones we see today. In Andorra-la-Vella we sought shade by the wall in the car park as we ate our lunch. We found the shops expensive and were happy to keep as cool as possible. Afterwards we made our way up into the mountains with the Andorrans leading. They looked for all the world that they were riding a horse as they effortlessly threw their Gold Wings around the steep, sharp bends. The road ran along the ski-lift cables, so you can imagine how high up it was. Unfortunately, we could not go right to the top as the clouds closed in and, as we went high through El Serrat, the rain started and almost at the top of the mountain (seven thousand feet up) on switchback roads, our Andorran friends turned us around as a little higher up it was snowing. On the downward ride I noticed that the ski-chairlifts were parallel with the road! Fighting nausea and hanging on while offering up a prayer, *(Ned was OK he was concentrating and in control)* we got down to Ordino in driving rain. Do not forget that at this point, we were still novices in this type of riding. The planned route back, took us around the back of another mountain and northwards to Soldeau, thus avoiding Andorra la Vella. (Suffice to say that I could only pen this part of the story once I had had a brandy and stopped shaking). Onwards and upwards through a pine clad mountain through thunder, lightning and hailstones and with flooding on the hairpin bends we dodged the stones which were being washed down to the road. Ned wears spectacles and had to have his visor up as he was steaming up and he could not see in the rain. By now he was also covered in rain and he had to take off his spectacles at one point! He kept his eye firmly on the Winger in front of us who seemed more confident and experienced than we were. All the blessings of Lourdes must still have been with us. Surely it was the hand of God which kept us safe. Arriving back at the hotel, Ned put his baby in the heated garage, emptied his pockets of water and hung up our riding gear nearby to dry off. As they were of breathable fabric it did not take long but those who wore leathers had wet gear for two days and those who had set out in shorts and tops got very wet as there was not time to put on riding gear in the suddenness of the weather change. In fact, some did not have any with them to put on. Due to the intense heat, Ned had been riding with his jacket open and his pockets unbuttoned. They became full of water, completely drowning the remote alarm key which he had kept there. As luck would have it, one of the Wingers had a tool kit with which he was able to undo it to dry out. We warmed up with hot drinks and brandies to settle our nerves. In the evening, the photo call was on the local News, showing our leader doing his 'birdie' act while riding his Gold Wing down the street. (Look! no hands, no feet!).

Monday brought the planned run through Pas de la Casa high in the mountains north into France, then south into Spain and Valle de Nuria. We travelled along double switchback roads and through spectacular scenery when the low clouds allowed. Ned rode solo for full concentration and I hitched a lift in a car (I promise, I had not lost my nerve). This also allowed me to capture on film the long line of Wings as they swooped around the bends through the valley. At Ribes de Freser we parked at the railway station and went up the mountain on the only rack railway of its kind in Spain. Due to low cloud we were unable to see as much of the valley as our organisers had hoped but we were able to see enough to get a flavour of what it was like. Ned, my engineer and mentor patiently explained to me thus:

'As the climb is so steep it is impossible to get traction. So a rack is built. This is actually rack and pinion and the rack is made up of what look like teeth. The pinion is a cogwheel, which fits into the rack as the driving force and is usually placed in the middle of the undercarriage. In this way it is possible to climb a forty five degree gradient.'

At Nuria there is a Sanctuary and until the rack railway was built, there was no access to this beautiful valley. Today, pilgrims come to stay in the apartment buildings. In the small and very simple but beautiful Church at 5.000 ft up you feel very close to God. The journey back to Soldeau from Ribes de Freser was full of contrast as we literally came down from the clouds and wound our way through mountain passes, crossing Spanish & French & Andorran borders back to our hotel.

We spent Tuesday and Wednesday with short rides out on our own, shopping and relaxing with the excellent fitness facilities in the hotel plus a spot of walking. We also saw a lovely ring in Encamp which was a more realistic price than those in the jeweller's shops in Andorra-la-Vella. As my wedding finger is slightly webbed there isn't much room for a third ring and so I have to wear it on my middle finger. I believe that one of my Irish great-grandfathers had webbed hands and this must be a relic of this. Ned, no bad Irish jokes please!

Thursday provided another highlight as today's ride out took us back along Pas de la Casa, into France on the Perpignan road and along the Tet Valley, to Villefranche de Conflet. Villefranche de Conflet is an old lived-in medieval town; again intact. The underground caves go back to the time when the Pyrénées Mountains were formed. They contain beautiful formations of stalactites and stalagmites. We went into the caves, where there were lighting effects and beautiful haunting music played. We spent a happy few hours wandering around, enjoying lunch and a chat. The roads were surprisingly good, much better than ours for the classification and if the trip had not been a planned one, I think that these two novices to European touring would have thought twice of using these roads. As it was, we learned to be a bit more adventurous and saw some wonderful sights. We headed back ahead of the main party in order to dodge the rainclouds which appeared over the mountains. What a deluge on the Pass over Puymorens! What happened to visibility over Pas de la Casa as we rode through the clouds? We could hardly see the road in front of us and it was a bit scary as we feared for our safety on this deserted, narrow, mountain road. Arriving back at our hotel, we dried off and by the time the rest of the party arrived, the rain had stopped, the clouds lifted and sunshine was again the order of the day. The outdoor hot tub was in great demand.

Following a party night and a relaxing sunbathing day on Friday, we headed for home on Saturday. Most of the group took the direct route westwards to the ferry ports but we were different as we wanted to see more of France. So, after an amazing out-of-this-world week we set out in bright sunshine for our journey back over the Pas de la Casa before turning eastwards, via the road tunnel, through Font-Romeu and Bourg-Madame, to travel along the Tet Valley to continue our discovery of France. We planned to then turn north towards Lyon and go via Reims to Calais.

We stopped to take one last photo of the Circle of Mountains, nine thousand feet high. *They looked so pretty against the bright blue sky with the fresh sprinkling of snow on the top and the fluffy white clouds circling the top of the mountains at the side.* We soon realised, that we were to ride through these as we climbed higher over the Pass. At this point we were very frightened as we could hardly see in front of us and Ned did not really know where he was going as we had missed a turning and the road somehow brought us back on ourselves. Visibility was again poor—but God was good—a Camper Van appeared in front of us from out of no-where, to guide us over and down the tortuous roads of the mountain. Ned thought that the driver seemed to know where he was going so he followed him! As we were heading towards Perpignan to travel back through the Rhône Valley, there was another Pass to negotiate. We did what is always advisable in these situations and followed a bus! Was our Guardian Angel working overtime? We then went through the tunnel in the mountain and came out into bright sunshine in what seemed a different world, leaving the mountains above and behind us. This part of our journey was definitely on a prayer!

The journey through the Tet Valley to Perpignan and then northwards via Lyon to Chalons sur Saône was beautiful. After stopping at Ville Franche de Conflet for coffee we turned towards Perpignan.

We had planned two alternative routes for this leg to Perpignan but after travelling this way on a run-out, we had no qualms about taking this beautiful scenic route. The Tet Valley runs through and along the bottom of the Pyrénées and is a must for a return trip to explore the area. We passed through a gorge, were the birds soared lazily in the cloudless blue sky while we soared below them until we hit the motorway at Perpignan, which passes along the eastern coast and turned north towards Narbonne and Lyon. The A9/E15 took us through the poppy fields—just as the Monet paintings show them—and then revealed a glimpse of the French Alps in the distance to the east. (This set Rosie's imagination running riot as she pointed them out to Ned. She felt another voyage of discovery coming on …). After negotiating Lyon we stopped overnight in Chalon sur Saône. We had pre-booked all the hotels, guaranteeing the room with our credit card, so we did not have a panic on to find something. The last lap of the journey to Calais, via Reims, was very windy. In fact the wind buffeted us for 400 miles and we rode most of the journey leaning to the left. All in all, this was an indication of the state of the weather at home. Worn out from battling with the strong winds on Sunday, (four hundred gruelling miles bending one way), we had rested in Calais, before boarding the train on Monday, back to England, the green hills of Wales and home.

Arriving earlier than planned at the Chunnel Terminal the following morning, we presented our tickets at the booth whereupon the attendant invited us to catch the train about to depart. We eagerly accepted this as we still had 300 miles to go at the other side in the UK. They are very relaxed about this on both sides of the channel. This method of travel is hassle free and as easy as pie for the bike as the ramps are short and quite flat. During the short journey we drew breath and had time to reflect on our contrasting experiences over the previous seventeen days, most of which I had caught on camcorder ready for editing into a film. We had travelled the length and width of France, coast to coast and north to south on both the west and east sides. The motorways were excellent, tollbooths easy to use with credit cards for payment and the service stations clean and reasonably priced.

A total journey of almost three thousand miles, and it is thanks to the two couples who organised the whole week that we had such a wonderful Gold Wing Andorran experience of discovery and adventure. It was not only on a Wing but on lots of prayers!

Reflections.

We had certainly travelled more than miles, in terms of new experiences and challenges and reflected that we would certainly go to Andorra again one day as there is so much still to see. This trip, although very stretching and initially daunting, gave us a good grounding for the future adventures and discoveries which our imaginations devised and the confidence to undertake them. We now eagerly looked forward to our next planned trip for 2001. (*This originally was to be the length and breadth of Italy travelling over the Alps and along the coasts bordering the Adriatic and Tyrrhenian Seas. However Ronda in Andalucia called and, as we had previously travelled through Italy on the train from Venice through Florence and Rome to Sorrento, Sunny Spain it was to be*). Well done Ned!

Leaving Soldeau, Andorra, 2000

Soldeau, Andorra
The road is level with with the Cable Car Lift to take skiers to the start of the ski runs

Andalucían Adventure

From coast to coast to follow a dream.

Following this epic journey into France and Andorra, Ned was working hard to make sure that the Wing was ready for 'the season'. He was determined to win the trophy again for joining the most ride-outs which took place in our region throughout the season. These were varied and I did not always go along as I was finishing my studies and catching up with the grandchildren. We went on a Riders Skills Workshop in May 2001 which was run by a member of North Wales Police and gives the tuition/assessment which the Police Riders have and a one to one riding session and feedback with a Policeman. They mainly do this in their own time. Photos of the weekend were posted onto the North Wales Wings very excellent web site. As we were about to embark on our big trip into the interior of Spain, it was reassuring to hear from the experts that Ned's riding was good. We knew that but it was good to hear. That year, I made a career change to look for a more local base and I also needed study time. I was kept busy researching for interview presentations …

I had longed dreamed of visiting Andalucía. Ever since my schooldays when I had been taught Spanish by a very inspiring teacher. One who taught us not only the grammar and language but, also brought alive the culture and sights and sounds of the region as she brought into class: posters, laces, castanets, matador clothing, and other examples of the country where she had lived for a time. It was quite unusual in those days to have this aspect in a language lesson.

As we have said earlier, when we bought our bike we had plans to conquer the world and had intended this year to see the Italian Dolomites and the Lakes before riding down the back leg of Italy and across to Sorrento before journeying to Nice and Monaco, to fulfill another romantic dream. When Andalucía and more specifically Ronda called, we pushed all that to one side and we set out on what was to be a journey of three thousand seven hundred miles or, to put another way—five thousand, nine hundred and twenty kilometers.

Planning for our Andalucía trip followed the usual pattern of extensive research into the route, a search for hotels and detailed costs. We loved poring over maps, working out mileage and guessing what the roads would be like for a motorbike. I was busy on the Internet as I trawled through for hotels. Some of them had a map on the Internet which showed a street plan. Others faxed a map to me which allowed us to plan in fine detail our approach to the town. At this time Google Earth was not readily available but I used whatever sources of information I had to hand and Multi-map on the Internet. Dredging the depths of my memory for my long-forgotten Spanish and using a phrase book, we composed letters to the hotels and faxed them. One or two came back in English but for the others it was back to the phrase book in order to translate and compose replies. We used international chains for the other hotels so booking was easy there as they had a central reservation service.

I set up a spreadsheet on my computer to keep a track of estimated costs, meals, mileage and estimated length of journey 'legs' and planned stops, to make sure the journey was viable. We did this just before and over the Christmas season and we even had a Christmas card from one of the hotels we had booked into. In Spanish no less! With all this in place we felt confident that we had covered all angles. For this trip I decided to record our impressions and thoughts on a daily basis and have included the transcript from June 3rd–23rd, 2001. In addition, as has become my habit, I also planned to film our travels for editing later. In June, the big day dawned and we set out for our trip which would realise a long held dream.

Monday 4th June. Morning.

'We got up bright and early yesterday (June 3rd) , earlier than planned, in order to get to the train terminal ready for the crossing to Calais and not lose the hour as much as we would have done if going later. The day was uneventful apart from going through London. We had to go through London to drop off a bag containing our evening clothes, at the hotel we were booked in for our return.'

It contained our posh clothes for our theatre visit and the City and Guilds Association Annual Dinner later in June.

'We turned off a little too early and found ourselves in the posh part of Belgravia in Cadogan Gardens and Eaton Square. Eventually, we calmed down; got back onto the bike and found our way out, went down Vauxhall Bridge Road and into Belgrave Road. We rode up and down and I got off to check the map against the directions. After asking a passer-by we found our hotel, Express by Holiday Inn, hoping the bags would be safe there until we came back. The receptionists were impressed with our planned tour—one of them came from Madrid and was quite impressed and excited with our itinerary. We then carried on to Folkestone for an overnight stop, dinner and early night.'

'We are looking forward to our journey through France today; the only trouble spot may be skirting Paris, due to the road network and hope that we do not end up in Paris. We should get into Orleans very easily. The plan is to take the A16 motorway from Calais, go down to Beziers, onto Beauvais and then, still on the A16, ride to J10 at Baumont onto the A184. This will take us nicely onto the N10 bypassing Versailles and heading towards Orleans and the A10. Then it would be time for a stop. We would then pick up A71 heading towards Clermont Ferrand for an overnight stop at the Holiday Inn Garden Court.'

Evening.

'Today was quite uneventful. The road was very long and very straight. The country is very large. The journey through France, took us through the centre of the country, skirting Paris and Versailles. The roads around here are a conglomeration with many changes. However, as we were not familiar with road signage and what would be the place to head for in order to join up with the one we wanted, we ended up outside the Palace of Versailles—on the cobbles! I had always wanted to see the Palace of Versailles and had been fascinated in history lessons of the pictures of life at court and the extravagant costumes which the courtiers wore. I had never envisaged that it would be in the centre of the city. We parked up the bike to look at the maps and stared fascinated at the palace which is huge. It curved around a massive courtyard on the town side and it would be nice to go inside one day. It is quite close to the railway station, so a trip from Paris would fit in very well as a day visit. That is, if I could ever get Ned to take me to Paris! Will that dream ever come true? Using my limited schoolgirl French, I asked a local for directions, using our Michelin Auto Routier and map. He was helpful until he realised that "je ne comprends pas" (I did not understand) and with an impatient shrug he thrust the maps back at me and walked off in disgust. We insisted to each other that we did not want the Paris signs but they all seemed to say Paris. What is one to do? We followed the road out and stopped at a petrol station where the helpful cashier soon explained the road marking to us. We were soon on our way out and onto the right road south to Clermont Ferrand.'

'We arrived in our hotel in Clermont Ferrand at about a quarter to seven in the evening after travelling about four hundred and fifty miles that day. The hotel was next to the Conference Centre and a good underground secure car park was within the hotel. We had to ask directions, as the town is larger than the maps indicated. With sign language, directions and a map, we and the Frenchman we stopped to ask, managed. As soon as I said the name of the Avenue, he was OK. The room at the Holiday Inn Garden Court was good and facilities excellent. Just what you need when you have been on a bike all day. I had slept most of the day (yes, on a bike), especially from Orleans down to Clermont Ferrand. It warmed up considerably now, the cold wind dropped and there was a nice warm breeze. The choice of wine for dinner reflects the change in the weather as we chose nice Rosé.'

Tuesday 5th June.
'We are looking at some sunshine now, it is twenty to eight on Tuesday morning, the sun is getting high in the sky and we are going to hit the road for Perpignan.'

Tuesday Evening over dinner... (Very tired). Ibis Hotel. Perpignan.

Rosie recorded the conversation and impressions over dinner:
'What a day!
"What did we do?"
Ned: "We started on the bike and finished up on the bike",
Rosie: "Yes, but what did we do in between?"
"We went ... Bzzzzzzzzzz Bzzzzzz," Ned replied.'

'It was lovely countryside with lots of yellow broom on the side of the motorway (yellow flowers). There was lots of motorway, then not motorway, and then it got quite exciting. Why was it? We were going through a town. It was bendy.'

"Oh those!" said Ned.'

'It was very like Andorra, the same sort of area, which was more south. Today was not as high up, but the road was quite sharp, only about eight hundred metres, approximately two thousand four hundred feet. Quite high though! And then it went down and down and a six percent drop and a then a seven percent drop. Also tunnels and ... (I don't think I went to sleep today).

Ned: "You had better put that in."

Rosie: "When we went up again and on to the top, it was not a patch on Denbigh Moors. Not how it was the other week. There is a lot of contrast between here and Denbigh Moors in North Wales."

Ned: "Yes, but it is harsh there. Nothing grows apart from bracken."

Rosie: "It is not so harsh here. It was tree lined, but those bends ... to, where was it, Millau?"

The service stations are excellent. We went down more motorways, down more bendy, bendy roads and then turned into Perpignan and stopped at a service station, to allow me to buy a map of the town.' *(The map for the hotel in the hotel guide was not quite clear as it turned out to be upside down and the hotel was easy to find!)*

Rosie continued:

'We rode along the motorway. There were lots of vines. The area is Languedoc Roussillon area (difficult to pronounce by now as sleep was catching up on me). All the fields were full of vines. It was quite uneventful and using the Ibis map we were looking ahead for the hotel. As we stopped in traffic on the bridge Ned told me through the intercom not to move as there was a steep camber and the bike was leaning alarmingly sideways. The lorry in front of us looked as if it was going to topple over. As we moved off again I gave a shout through the intercom:

"There it is, on the right".

The map was upside down! As the road into the town was on a big steep camber Ned had a job to hold up the bike.

"What would you have done if it had gone?" I asked later.

"We would have picked ourselves up! If it had gone the other way, we would have got run over!" Ned replied.'

'After a shower, change and a stroll round the town we rested on the riverside and then did a reccae of the road out for the following morning.

"Tomorrow is Valencia", I said. "We could buy a map. I am not convinced that all the maps tally up. We come off the A7, but we may have to come off that and go onto another one. I am not convinced it will be so easy." I commented.

Dinner was in the hotel and this is where we came unstuck again as the menu was in French only and the waiters did not speak English. I ordered salmon, not realising that smoked salmon was raw. The waiter tried to confirm that I really did want this but in my ignorance, I thought I did. That was catastrophe number one!'

'We had tomato soup with basil (not hot). Ned had marinated pork ribs; I had thinly sliced salmon covered with Dill and tomatoes. Ned had tarte pommes and I had trois fromage (It was one small thinly slice each of three cheeses. nothing else, no crackers.) It was all carbohydrate. (Giggling …).'

Wednesday and Thursday, Valencia.

The next morning we set off to join the Motorway which would take us towards Barcelona. This was an unexpectedly busy road, unlike most of the motorways in France. It is however to be expected as it is the main route across the French/Spanish border. By-passing Barcelona we continued down the coastal motorway to spend a couple of days in Valencia.

'Valencia is a charming city and we had booked into a new hotel on the eastern side of the city. I chose this as I thought it would be easier to find and yet did not seem too far out of the centre for exploring. Another attraction was the swimming pool and the hairdryer in the bedroom. As we approached the centre, we hit a big roundabout with six lanes of traffic and there was lots of traffic to integrate on the roundabouts. Not very clever when you don't know where you are going and everyone else does. The hotel was signposted on the main approach—helpful. What appeared on the map to be a river was actually the dried-up riverbed which was now a play area. The river had been diverted and that explained the map.'

As it was so hot we were looking forward to a dip in the pool but as we pulled up we could see that it was not yet commissioned as it was still being tiled. Ah well! Not to worry, a cool shower would have to do. The hotel was smart, sleek and modern but the restaurant was not yet open. The manager directed us around the corner to a little restaurant where the locals ate. At the time I recorded that it was:

"The Sacramento, which we went to on both nights. I had fish again, but was not yet growing gills! We enjoyed a good red wine both nights."

What a pleasant way to choose a meal. There was no menu. The owner asked us what we wanted to eat and he cooked it. We chose the wine from a rack on the wall. How civilized and unfussy.

'We went into the El Saler shopping centre next to the hotel. It was very big with lots of different restaurants and shops including a Carre Four supermarket which sells everything, where Ned bought some canvas shoes. I was tempted with a Flat Screen and Notepad Computer but I remained strong-minded!' 'We walked into Valencia and took a ride on the open-topped bus on Thursday and I got lots of film of the old city and the new re-generation. It was well worth the money. The commentary was in a variety of languages, with earphones provided. Clean ones every time. We sat on the top, underneath the awning at the back. The bus went round some streets a few times. There was a monastery here originally and they built the town around that. The bus went down to the new Oceanographic and Science Park. (Ned took photos later that day). There is going to be a Planetarium and a Sphere where you can see how the world evolved. They are still putting things in place and ever optimistic they put places on the map which they have not yet built. The open-topped bus ride was well worth it as we found out a lot in the short time we had here in this delightful city. I had hoped to buy some Valencian lace, but there didn't seem to be any lace shops.—never mind!'

Friday 8th June. Paraiso del Mar, Nerja.
'What an amazing day! On the way out from the hotel in Valencia, we ended up back in the city, (the signposts are designed for locals), and skirted the southern part into the busy commercial area, in the early rush hour. We picked up the motorway on the west side of the city, stopping at a petrol station on the way. We followed the coast road on the motorway past Alicante to Murcia. The central reservations are full of colourful flowering shrubs and very pretty. A couple of Gold Wings passed us and we reflected that they must be on their way to the Spanish Treffen. As we rode along high above the coast and sandy beaches below, we could see the sea sparkling in the sun and the tall high-rise hotels ranged along the coastal resorts like soldiers. We turned inland at Murcia towards Guadix and Granada to go over the sierras north of Sierra Nevada. (I just wanted the experience and what an experience!). We did about three hundred and seventy miles that day. It was very hot and amazing going over the sierras. The earth which appeared to be scorched red was not only deserted, but hot. Hot and barren, with only the occasional vehicle passing us. For the most part we were the only people in sight in this barren silent area with only mountains for company. I wondered what secrets they held. Ned was worried about the petrol situation and when we saw a roughly made sign-post by the side of the road with 'Services' carved into it, pointing over into the hills in the distant yonder, he was ready to turn off the road and follow it but I had a bad feeling.

"No, no Ned! We are not turning off the road into the distant hills. We don't know what is over there. It could be bandits. It could be a trap and we could be ambushed." I shouted into the intercom.

I strongly advised Ned to only stop if we could actually see a building (not a shack!). Reluctantly, Ned heeded my warning and concern but he really was worried about running out of petrol when he saw what was on the petrol gauge. All at once I shouted:

"Over there!"

I had seen a Shell Petrol Station right on top by the roadside—just like in the old adverts of the American West. Thankfully, we pulled in and Ned filled up with petrol before parking the bike under the covered parking area. We found that this was a feature of Spain. I selected sandwiches and cold drinks from the shop. Uncannily, the lay out was just the same as in the United Kingdom so I felt quite at home. We sat outside under the umbrellas and as we rested and watered, observing that there was not much traffic. Ned said that he had not felt so hot since his overalls had caught fire once so that gives you some idea of the heat that day. We also agreed that we were glad of our breathable Cordura jacket and trousers, under which you can wear as much or as little as you wish, and were glad that we were not wearing leathers.'

We also reflected how brave we were riding through this beautiful but deserted and lonely area—just us two—when we didn't know what perils could befall us. What an exciting adventure! What use is a mobile phone anyway, when you either don't speak Spanish or it is very limited? We really were relying on our inner resources.

'On reaching Granada we turned south to the coast and Motril. I had hoped to have seen the Alhambra Palace in the distance as we skirted the city but we were too far away. The countryside now was more interesting, with lots of steep drops and bends. The sun was high in the sky and, although most sensible people in this part of the world take a siesta to escape from the heat, we were conscious of the distance we still had to travel to Nerja and so ploughed on. As we rode through this beautiful green area it became hotter and hotter. We rode through deserted and sleepy villages (all sensible people were inside). The sun shone in a clear blue sky through tall, oh so green, trees which made dappled shadows across the road as we swooped along. We travelled alongside a river that sparkled in the sun as it wended its way down this beautiful Lecrin Valley to be released into the warm lazy waters of the Mediterranean Sea.'

'By now it was mid afternoon and the sun was climbing ever higher in the sky. Petrol was once again getting low as were our personal water reserves. Ned had to constantly monitor the petrol situation as the petrol tank on a motorbike is more limited than that of a car. Dropping down through this green and leafy valley, we espied a petrol station and prayed that it was open. If we had run out of petrol heaven knows what we would have done. I was impatient to remove my helmet and as Ned 'watered the beast', in other words, filled up with petrol, I dashed into the cool darkness of the interior and desperately asked for:

"Agua, por favor?" I gasped. ("Water, please?").

Oh, the relief as I saw a huge chiller chest full of beautiful bottles of ice-cold water. Quickly purchasing our supplies we slaked our thirst and commented that the couple who were sleeping in the car parked under the trees had the right idea. We were not really 'tuned in' to siesta time. Travelling on, the countryside was increasingly more interesting with lots of steep drops and bends as we neared the sea.'

'We picked up the coast road again and turned west to ride above Salobreña with the sea on our left. Oh! How charming this was as we rode above the rocky coast with its inlets and beaches below. Passing through tunnels cut into the rock we reached the open road above Almuñecar and headed down for the last short leg to Nerja. We looked out for signs for the Parador as the hotel was next to this, overlooking the Burriana beach. We had a little adventure as we followed the town map I had pulled off the Internet. We could see the road we wanted as we came into the town.'

'By now we were down by the beach and were next to the hotel but did not know it. We followed the narrow roads and the hotel signs (In Spain/France, all towns have their hotels signposted).

"Look! There is the Parador! We are right next to it!" I shouted through the intercom.'

'Disaster now befell us! The road in front of us was fenced off with a wire fence. It was a building site but, wait, the gate was open so Ned rode through onto the rubble. Do not forget that the Gold Wing was fully laden and weighed half a ton so it took some expertise to keep it upright in these conditions. I got off to do a reccae and walked across the site onto the road we wanted and excitedly found the hotel. Ned knew that the road was one way and could not turn round to go back but, in any case, he said that he was not going to try and manoeuvre and turn round risking damage so, he simply rode across ignoring the lone worker who quickly shut the gate behind us! (We found out later that the one-way restriction had been cancelled). Ned quickly parked up in front of the charming hotel of Moorish style and we went into the

Just Us Two

cool quiet interior. Through an archway we could see the sea. This was paradise, with a beautiful family owned hotel right by the beach and sea. What excellent accommodation!'

'The receptionist was excited when she heard that we had a Gold Wing and, leaving me to register, dashed out to have a look and drool. Coming back she showed us to our accommodation. The hotel may have been a private house. We had booked the first two nights in an annexe which was another small house and definitely private. Situated next door, this building was incorporated into the hotel. The suite was the whole ground floor, bedroom, half glass doors into the sitting/dining room, breakfast room and bathroom with Jacuzzi. On the terrace a marble table with chairs sat in the shade waiting for us. This terrace led onto the upper lawn and the steps down to the sea. The pool was on the lower level in front of the main hotel in-between the terrace and overlooking the sea. As Ned continued to carry in the bags and secure the bike, I left my unpacking to strip off and finding a costume made straight for the pool. As Ned came past with the last of the bags I shouted:

"It is lovely in here!"

He laughed in amazement but soon joined me.'

Nerja is a beautiful place and Rosie continues her recorded narration:

'We had a walk around that evening stopping at a restaurant overlooking the sea for dinner. On Saturday we had a good time exploring and went on the little train, 'El Tren' which was fun. We saw more than we would have done if we had walked. Down a narrow street a fruit and vegetable wagon backed into the little train when they got stuck. El Tren was bruised and battered and then the train knocked down a signpost at a road junction. This was soon fixed as they just bent it back up. Simple really! The Spanish people are all so laid back and relaxed. The singing family in front was annoying! We strolled along the promenade built along the edge with passages cut through the rocks. Sometimes a passage seemed impossible, but Ned found a way. There were some lovely views of little coves and views across the sea around the coast and we came up near our hotel to a little café for a cold drink. We arrived back at the hotel and went down to the sea for a little dip picking up pebbles for our grandchildren. Our next mission was to collect the laundry which we had deposited earlier and there was no language problem here as a Scotsman ran the laundry. On Sunday we strolled into town early for Mass at 11am before having a nice lunch and a quiet afternoon. As arranged, due to previous bookings, the third night was a room in the main hotel. The transfer was easy. Nerja truly is paradise!'

Monday 11th June. Ronda. Hotel La Espanola.
The next leg of our journey was to ride along the coast, via Marbella and up into the hills to Ronda.

'We set off early while it was cool. It was only a hundred miles to Ronda. Using the motorway we rode from Nerja and after negotiating the heavy early morning traffic around Malaga, rode high above Marbella in the early morning sun. Passing a still sleeping Marbella we turned at San Pedro de Alcántara for the climb to Ronda. It was even better than we remembered! The road was bendy to say the least! By this I mean that there were switchback roads as we climbed higher and higher. We didn't go through the clouds as we did last time on the bus but there were a few specs of rain. It is very high up there going through the passes and quite windy at some points. From our ever-higher vantage point we could see across the valley down to the coast below and felt on top of the world. Unlike the sierras in the south east, the mountains here were green with many trees shading the road and steep drops.'

After looking at the map of Malaga later I can now recount that we came off the motorway at San Pedro to pick up the A376 mountain road through the Sierra Palmitera on our right and the Sierra Bermeja on our left. There is a viewpoint at Puerto de Alijar at 1410 metres and another where the road winds around the Cascajares Mountain. Here you are looking back to the sea from whence you have come and across to the Serrania de Ronda in the north.

'On approaching Ronda we could see it nestling in the sunshine and red earth. The countryside unfolded before us and there was hardly a soul about at this point. Approaching the town and crossing the bridge over the gorge we passed the main square and the Parador which overlooks the gorge. As we did so, using the map which the hotel had faxed me and a map off the Internet, I caught sight of the sign of our hotel sign swinging from the entrance.

Just Us Two

"There it is," I shouted excitedly to Ned through the intercom, "over there!"

"Where?" Ned asked impatiently. "Over there is no good."

"On the left just ahead," I replied resignedly.

I could see the hotel tucked away down a narrow shady street off the end of the square. At the other end of the street near the gardens, as we were to discover, was the second oldest bullring in Spain and one of the most beautiful. It was now 11:00am and it was very, very hot. By 11:30am we had unpacked settled in and went off into the town to explore. It was a lovely old hotel. The bedrooms are very ornate and traditional, with cutwork curtains. We had to go across the narrow street to the other hotel for a breakfast which was not as varied as in Nerja. The waiters go back and to between the hotels as they are worked as one. The narrow street was very shady with lots of tables and umbrellas from the hotels set out for weary, footsore wanderers. We had dinner the first night in a terrace restaurant overlooking the gorge. This was the stuff of dreams; a travel-guide come true. As we relaxed over dinner, we reflected with a huge, huge sigh of satisfaction and sense of achievement that we 'had done it'. We had made it to this southernmost part of Spain into the unknown, to realise a dream and that from now on it was homeward bound. We went around the old historic part. We didn't need a guide (last time we were taken around by a local who 'fleeced' us for money as he had five children! How naïve we were then). This time we weren't to be caught out and explored on our own. It was nice having been there before as we were able to see more than we would have done if it had been our first visit.' *(Some years ago there was a TV advert which showed a little lad, with a hole in his bucket, drawing water from a water pump that has a lot of taps. Ned says that this was taken in Ronda as we stood right by an identical water pump. He is probably right.)*

Our first stop was the Tourist Information Office and we made good use of the maps to explore. We are quite close to the gorge and the old Roman and Arabian bridges.'

What tales they could tell, what secrets they must hold. For those of you who don't know, Ronda is a lovely old Roman/Arabian town built across a gorge in the mountains of Andalucía. (The local tale is that God made the gorge to separate the men and the women).

Tuesday 12th June. Day 9 of our Andalucían Adventure.
Rosie continues her recorded narration:

'We enquired about laundry. The laundry/dry cleaning shop is quite close to the hotel and offers a good service. We went to the railway station to enquire about trains to Algeciras. Ronda is situated on the Guadiaro River and the trains runs through the town from Granada, down the mountains, through the famous Pueblos Blanco's (white villages) to Jimena de la Frontera and down to Algeciras on the coast. The boats go from there to Tangier. We go there tomorrow—but not on the Andalucía Express as it leaves too early.'

'The streets in this part of Ronda are lined with orange trees, full of ripe, juicy oranges. It was tempting to pick one! Outside the Police Station in the town, there are lots of orange trees in front of the ornate building. We thought that we had better not pick an orange in case a policeman was watching. We had another good explore and spent some time in the shady park enjoying ice creams. We walked along the promenade along the edge of the gorge. It is amazing and we thought that it would be nice to walk down into it.'

Wednesday 13th June. Algeciras.
Today it was thirty-four degrees centigrade and the cooling breeze and shady trees were welcome.

'The contrast in scenery from when we came across to Granada is truly amazing. As the train wended its way down the mountainside through the valley and tunnels, it stopped many times for locals to embark and disembark. The train was like a bus really and probably the main means of transport. The rivers run down the mountain and down either side are lovely pink flowers. It was a fascinating journey and we were lost in wonder and anticipation of what we would find at the other end.

Algeciras looked poor and dusty and in need of some renovation. We found our way into the centre and stopped at a café in the square. The people seemed wary and we sipped our cold drinks quickly. I was enchanted with the gold and blue tiles which adorned the seats flowerbeds in the centre of the square. The patterns were quite intricate. The railway is in the Port part of town where there a lots of travel agents

Just Us Two

for passages to Tangier. There are many single men strolling around and later, across the road some groups of men who appeared to be stalking us. Ned said to keep on walking and just act normally as one passed us and stopped to use his mobile phone to someone up front/or back. I kept my hand on my belt-bag and tried hard not to turn around as this would have raised suspicions. We saw a well-dressed young lady and man and her baby, who had been begging earlier in the town and Ned thought they could be part of the stalking group. The men melted away at the Port entrance where the security posts were which was a great relief. We found our way into the main part of town, past the market and into the square with the gold and blue tiled flowerbeds and fountains. Heading to the park we found shade and coolness. The walk back along the sea front (lined with beautiful flowering trees) was quiet, too quiet. We decided not to linger and all in all, we were glad to get back on the train as it had been a quite hairy day but were glad of the experience of seeing the town and the journey down through the valley through the Pueblos Blanco's. Back in Ronda we sorted our laundry and dropped it off for collection later before enjoying another lovely meal to round off the day.'

The laundry solution is one which we picked up in Andorra and cuts down on luggage. Well, that is the theory anyway!

Thursday 14th June.

'We came onto the street at 10:00am and the sun 'smacked us in the face' it was so unbelievably hot. Stopping in the square outside the Parador we saw a mini-bus which advertised a photographic tour of the town and gorge. The tour took us around the old Arabic part of town before descending into the gorge. The driver stopped at intervals and explained the history of the town and gorge in addition to the commentary on board. Ned took lots of photos and I had the camcorder running the whole time. The driver took our photo with the bridge in the background and this provided a lasting memento of our adventure of discovery of what was, for us, an epic tour and as we look at it in its frame, we realise just how far we had travelled—in more ways than one. He had Spanish Music playing and the CD was on sale at the end.'

Between us we had some excellent shots and I was so enchanted with the whole experience of the gorge and the beautiful music that I insisted that we buy the CD. I also thought that the music would fit in nicely when I came to edit and make the camcorder film into a movie on the computer back home.

'This has been an amazing few days, with impressions jumbled around. It is a beautiful part of the country. Now it was time for dinner. Food, food and more food. It is half past seven and not a cloud in the sky. We are thankful for the air conditioning.'

All in all we felt that it had been worth the return journey to explore Ronda further than our previous day trip had allowed. Indeed, the journey here had been the pinnacle of our trip as we journeyed into the unknown.

Friday 15th June. Aranjuez.
(Recorded in San Sebastián)

'We had an early start to get inland to Aranjuez, south east of Madrid, before the heat built up. Our journey out of Ronda on the A-367 took us north to Campillos and Córdoba; east via Bailen before heading north again via Valdepeñas to Aranjuez—a total of three hundred and sixty miles. On leaving Ronda, we were entranced by the fields full of large sunflowers turning their faces to the rising sun and waving in the breeze as they nodded us on our way. They grew here as we grow corn in our fields in the United Kingdom. Our route was to take us by the lakes and we decided not to go on the little roads to Campillos, as they looked quite rough but one sign said Malaga and we thought:

"On no we don't want that one."

So we ended up on the little road which after all which took us around some lakes. The beauty here—where all the rivers flowing down from the mountains end their journey as they meet in the blue lakes glinting in the sunshine—was a totally unexpected surprise after the scorched earth near Granada and the expected rough surface of this road was not too bad after all although it *was* like riding through a ploughed field.'

'Although it was very, very, hot, we had an uneventful journey travelling north via Córdoba, where we joined the EO5, Bailen and Valdepeñas. The road in to Aranjuez went straight over cobbles. This called for some careful handling of the Wing as it was heavily loaded. Aranjuez is a very old town where the Spanish kings and queens had their summer palace. We found the hotel eventually, over the river unexpectedly, as the map did not have that street name over the river. It was good to have the Multimap copies as it was easy to get directions and we did have a nice ride over the cobbles. As Ned brought in the bags and I checked in I asked:

"Where is the pool?"

"The pool is not open. It is not summer," The receptionist replied.

"When is summer?" I queried in amazement.

"July, August," was the unconcerned reply.'

Not summer and it was scorching hot? It was unbelievable. Worse was to come:

"Is the café bar open? We need a cold drink," I continued.

It was like a pantomime as the receptionist replied:

"It is closed. Open when the pool is open."

So that was that. We were tired and thirsty and we could not even get a cold drink in this supposedly three star hotel. We would have to go out and find something.'

'I had forgotten that this was the only hotel without a hairdryer and having washed my hair, dried it under the air conditioning unit, thankful that I had the benefit of a good cut which fell into place with ease. After Ned had also showered we had a walk around the town and at the end of the street found a shop where we bought cold cans of cola. As we had no change we had to use a very large Peseta note which I think took all the change in the shop. It was a sleepy time of day and there were not many people about as we strolled where kings and queens had once spent their summers. The intricately designed stone buildings reminded me of those in Versailles in France. On balance, we decided to make a very early start in the morning to escape the heat and not to wait for breakfast as they did not serve it early enough. We bought supplies in the Shell Station across the road from the hotel and planned to set off at about 6:30am as we had a long journey in the morning of about three hundred and sixty miles to San Sebastian. The dinner in this three star hotel was mediocre and a disappointment. Suffice to say that this leg of the journey was memorable for all the wrong reasons but, you just have to laugh and notch up the experience.'

Saturday 16th June. San Sebastián. Hotel Ezezia.

'After a very early 6:00am start in the dark we headed for the motorway E90 towards Zaragoza, Pamplona and Donostia-San Sebastián for a two-night stay. We negotiated Madrid without too much trouble. However, we found we were heading south-west towards Toledo as we got onto the wrong motorway when we missed a sign completely, so we doubled back and followed the Valencia signs from where we were soon able to pick up the Zaragoza signs which would take us further north.. It was extremely cold as we travelled over the sierras and we thought it was because it was early. I had not realised that this part of Spain was so high up (four thousand feet).

The countryside was amazing, but we were very, very cold. It was a shock after the heat of the previous day but extremes of temperature are a feature of the area around Madrid which can vary by about fifteen degrees in a day. At our first stop near Zaragoza we warmed ourselves in the village café as the local men had their breakfast and we put our warm liners back into our jackets. We should have done this sooner. We were riding on top of the mountains—a plateau—and along with ruined castles in the distance we had windmills and radar masts for company. This was Castile country. There was very little on the roads and we just hoped that there were no bandits lurking around.'

'Riding along, I was able to reflect on the history lessons from my schooldays and all the queens who had come from Spain to England. This journey brought everything to life and, seeing the ruined castles, I could imagine the young princesses in them before they left for a strange country. It was do desolate and as it was so flat we did not realise that we were so high up and riding on a plateau.'

'Skirting Pamplona we came into the north. The mountains in northern Spain are high, about two thousand feet high, with deep lush, green valleys. As we came towards San Sebastián, we rode down and ever more downwards through a gorge. Would it never end? Would we ever come to civilisation? Now this *was* a match for North Wales. Beautiful!'

'In San Sebastián we ended up in the town and stopped to ask directions, using our town map. It is bigger than we thought. All signs are in Basque and Spanish. It was a Royal resort and the buildings are an indication of the prosperity of the town. The river runs in the middle of the two bays of the town, down into the sea which is quite active at this point. (The hotel was on the bay to the west of the town and, as we had come off at the wrong junction, we were on the La Concha beach and lost. After re-tracing our steps we found the right road to the hotel.) Later, we became drenched while we walked along eating our ice creams, as the sea comes in with big breakers. It reminded us of Blackpool in the North of England, noted for being windy. We managed to buy stamps for the cards we had written for our grandchildren. The Post Office had moved, but we found the Tabaco in one of the narrow streets. We were lucky as it was nearly 5:00pm on a Saturday'.

'The hotel is on the Ondaretta beach but the restaurant was not open and there was no explanation. We went to the San Marco along the road for a meal. This was a private villa which still contains the original furnishings with brass carvings and candlesticks on the piano and a Lalique chandelier. We had an excellent meal and if we had not gone so early, would not have got a table as it was so popular.'

Sunday 17th June.

'We went on the open-topped bus tour after Mass. The commentary was in various languages and as we went around the town on both sides of the river we heard about its history. The bus also went up to Monte Igueldo where there were some fantastic views of the bay with La Concha beach which is shaped like a conch shell. The buildings are beautiful, with a beautiful Cathedral. It is beautiful everywhere and very ornate. The beach is beautiful and clean. The beach on the other side has lots of surfers.

After the tour we strolled along and in the gardens in the centre of town there was an orchestra playing with couples dancing along. It was like a tea dance but at lunchtime and was a charming sight. There was a carousel in the square for the children who rode up and down with happy smiles and squeals as it played its merry music. It started to rain and as it was Sunday and the weather was turning chilly, we treated ourselves to Sunday lunch at a smart hotel on the sea front—near the royal bathing huts—while the weather cleared. It got cold in the evening and dinner that night was on the covered terrace of the hotel as the locals were watching football in the main bar.'

Some things do not change when it comes to football.

Monday 18th June.

This last leg will take us from San Sebastián along the A8 over the border into France onto the A10, past Bordeaux to Niort. From there we planned to stay in Nantes and the Holiday Inn Garden Court.

'The journey to Nantes was uneventful. Leaving San Sebastian we quickly found the motorway and negotiated the tolls as we went along. There was nobody on the border post who wanted to look at our passports as they simply waved us through. The motorway northwards was in flat country. The hotel again was on a map which did not show exactly how the road would lead you in to the town. The hotel was beautiful, modern, new, and they sent up to our room a tray of exotic soft fruits and chilled water, which was very welcome.

Following our usual pattern of unpack, shower and explore, we took a quick tour of Nantes. The river Loire splits into two and the hotel is on a small island in the middle, but a good location. The tram system is good with frequent trams which have right of way over other traffic. My schoolgirl French was enough for us to get directions to the city centre, also to find a Tabac. We bought and posted another post card to our grandchildren.

These postcards have mapped the journey for them and allowed us to share our travels with them as we went along. Anyway, they would be missing us. We had a lovely meal in the hotel and did our usual reccae of the road out ready for the morning.'

Tuesday 19th June. St. Omer. Hotel Ibis.

Rosie again recorded the day:

'After Ned got the bike out of the garage and loaded up, we left Nantes, riding over the bridge across the river and eastwards towards Anger and Orleans, before turning north towards Versailles, Paris and St Omer (outside Calais). We picked up the motorway and lost the motorway. We had a detour at one point which is quite a worry when you are low on petrol and, at one point, Ned was sure that we were going round in circles as we followed the detour signs. At Le Mans we decided not to risk Versailles and the Paris outskirts, but instead turned north towards Rouen and St Omer as it was as broad as long.

Just Us Two

The hotel was quite central but not as modern as others we had stayed in. We explored and enjoyed a couple of drinks at pavement cafes in the square while we admired the buildings and people watched.

We posted the last postcard to our grandchildren. It is a nice little town and, as is common in Europe, they flew the flag over the Town Hall. We reflected that if we were travelling eastwards from Calais, this town would be a good overnight stop as it is only ten miles from Calais.'

The Gorge in Ronda

Ned and Rosie Safely in Nerja

Royal Palace in Aranjuez, Madrid, Spain

Donostia - San Sebastian
on the North Coast of Spain
from Monte Igueldo

Wednesday 20th June. Calais to London.

The headphones on the helmets are partly what makes touring enjoyable as you can chat about things. However they are not always a blessing. Especially not when you hear a very, very, loud voice in your helmet, shaking you out of your reverie.

Rosie continues her narration:

'It was not far to Calais, but the signposting was a little hit and miss and caused a problem, in that we didn't agree what the signposts had said. This caused a little contremps between us and the sound of my sobbing down the intercom culminated in my pulling out my intercom plug!

"Speak to me Rosie," Ned shouted desperately.

(Ned could not speak any French and understood even less). But of course I could not hear. Eventually I relented and I restored normal communication channels by plugging back in.

"That will teach you to shout at me Ned!" I retorted.'

'We arrived early at the station and got on an earlier train. I directed us along a nicer route into London, by going further west along the M25 into Surrey. This would give Ned a flavour of this part of the country as the view across the downs as you head towards the M25 is stupendous. All my workday travels were coming useful as I know most of the England.'

'We found our hotel easily and our bag was safe! What relief there was as we retrieved our bag of posh clothes as we had paid a lot of money for my new feathers, and of course, shoes! Ned went off to collect his suit from Moss Bros and we were all set for our City&Guilds Dinner the following night. We took a tube to Green Park and had a lovely late lunch in Henry's Café Bar on Piccadilly before changing for the theatre. Mama Mía was a fantastic show! Superb! Well worth the money! It was as good as, and better than, the reviews and we all ended up on our feet at the end as we joined in with 'Super Trouper'. We went to a café afterwards and met up with an American couple, who shared our table as it was so busy. They live and work on opposite seaboards. He in New York at Yale University (Professor of Surgery according to his card) on the east and she lives in California. The both travel and meet up as and when. I promised to e-mail details of Nerja.'

(This meeting was a strange event as I work in Yale College in Wrexham and Elihu Yale, an original benefactor of Yale University in America, is buried in the Parish Churchyard in Wrexham as he came from that area. Yale University has a replica of the Parish Church Tower [one of the Seven Wonders of Wales] on its campus).

Thursday 21st June. London.
Rosie explains:

'We walked along the river and took a trip on the London Eye before walking up the Mall, onto Piccadilly and lunch again at Henry's Café Bar. The City&Guilds Dinner in the city was excellent. We were dressed up to the nines. We had arrived in biking gear and as we tripped out of the hotel—I in a new long cream dress with a slit up the side teamed with a Guipure lace jacket and gold zebra- stripe shoes and Ned in dinner jacket and black tie—I could not help reflecting what a contrast we made to the biker image!' It just goes to show that you can't make assumptions or judge a book by its cover.

The following morning we packed up our glad rags and, with a huge sigh of satisfaction at what we had achieved, kitted ourselves up in our riding gear ready for the last two hundred miles home. All in all it was a stupendous trip of approx. three thousand seven hundred miles. This 'out of this world' adventure was at times: scary, covered a wide spectrum of demanding dramatic Spanish terrain, embraced extremes of heat and cold, demanded much of the Gold Wing which did not let us down, and stretched us to the limit as we plunged into the deep well of our inner resources, relying only on each other in a strange country with limited Spanish as we travelled—just us two—and proved that dreams can come true.

You too can follow your dream but sometimes you just have to give things a helping hand.

Closer to Home

Over the hills in search of ice-cream

This year (2002) was uneventful, compared to last year as we concentrated on riding in the United Kingdom.

Enjoying spring and summer at home.
We spent time in the spring and summer riding to various places in England and Wales. It is true to say that we saw more of Wales in 2002 than we had since leaving Lancashire in 1967. One feature of ride-outs is that we have to search for that ever-elusive ice cream. Not your usual run of the mill version but homemade luscious ice cream. We went on all the ride-outs and one memorable one took us to Mumbles near Swansea for ice cream. It was a very expensive ice cream. There were just 3 Wings—quite a nice small number for a ride-out of this magnitude—riding south towards Newtown before heading westwards towards the coast in Mid Wales. Then our leader took us through some spectacular scenery and roads towards South Wales and Mumbles where, after buying our ice cream, we relaxed near the water's edge eating it as we watched people messing about with boats. Mumbles is a delightful place and the whole day was one to treasure in our memory box of adventures.

One Sunday ride-out was to the Welsh Castles. Travelling along the A55 we passed Bodelwyddan, Gwrych, Penrhyn and Conwy castles before re-grouping at Caernarfon Castle. Moving on to Barmouth along the coast we stopped for ice-cream and lunch before travelling via Porthmadog to Harlech were the group split up as 'some took the high road and some took the low road'. The CB radios came into their own as there were calls of 'where are you?' Passers-by and tourists in this ancient sleepy town were astounded by all this activity during this invasion of bikers. (One can't help reflecting how the outcome of battles in days gone by could have been changed if the soldiers and invaders had had CB Radios to check progress of the battle). Eventually we all caught up with each other. Unfortunately, the group separated as we came back onto the narrow main road and one in front turned the wrong way. After shouts down the CB the first one turned quickly into a steep track across the road to go in the right direction. The bike behind was ridden by one of our new Wingers who, on attempting the same manoeuvre had a spill as he dropped the bike on the tight turn into this uphill sidetrack. Apart from embarrassment, this is not too bad for the rider but nerve-racking for the passenger especially when you are only just getting used to riding pillion. It was not a turn to attempt lightly and fortunately, we had not yet hit the road and knew which way we were going.

A shorter run took us to Ellesmere in Shropshire via Ruthin, Nant-y-Garth Pass, Horseshoe Pass and Llangollen and down to Chirk and Oswestry. We intended to feed the ducks on the Mere—after ice cream and tea of course—but as we parked up outside the little tea shop the owner, with frantic waving of arms, banned us from coming in as we had not given twenty four hours notice and he had enough bikers in already. No amount of remonstrating with him changed his mind. When you think of the total value of all the Gold Wings there, plus chrome and lights well, I mean, you are not going to cause any trouble are you, especially when you have a police sergeant among you. The Little Chef a few miles down the road later made us very welcome and soothed our battered pride.

We continued to raise money for our named charity by having a static display in a shopping centre and had a run to Devil's Bridge in Aberystwyth which we reached after riding over the Llandegla Moors to Llangollen and Newtown before turning west. We had a good look at the waterfall after enjoying our lunch.

Another ride out was to Hawkstone Park in Shropshire where we met up with another region. The idea was to have a 'shared lunch' where we all took a dish and had a dip into everything as the fancy took you. After lunch we strolled through the extensive parkland and follies which were amazing and involved some quite strenuous climbs. Again the glorious weather made the day.

We wanted to have a short break in June but could not get a flight and so booked a couple of nights in County Durham. We travelled there after the regional run-out to Southport on the west Lancashire coast (where it rained all the way). As this run had started off after our monthly meeting, it was getting quite late in the afternoon before we stopped and I was cold and tired as riding in the miserable rain for a long period is not much fun for a pillion passenger. Breaking away from the group and riding east ahead of the rain we soon found and settled into our country hotel where we had booked a couple of nights. The village nearby was charming and as we strolled around we watched them set up the Hog Roast for the Queen's Jubilee on the Bank Holiday Monday. Later that evening we watched the 'Party at the Palace' on a wide screen TV in the hotel.

Wing Ding-ing.

In July we had our Wing Ding in Ruthin, North Wales. A Wing Ding, is advertised essentially as a camping event which regions of the Club hold every two years. Our region had usually held it at a Rugby Club as they had a good field and a good clubhouse for entertainment and facilities.

It was central to the lovely ancient town of Ruthin and by following the path from the field, crossing the river you soon found yourself near the old castle, gaol and the winding streets with their black and white beamed buildings dating back to the 16th Century. The town is full of antique shops, craft shops and all the other shops and hotels you would hope to find in a bustling market town. There is always a good, well-planned, ride-out on the Saturday to take in the wonderful scenery and biking roads which Wingers from all over the country come to our Wing Ding for.

Ned and I were Marshalls on what was a memorable ride out to Portmeirion (near Porthmadog) on the west coast of Wales. Portmeirion of course is the Italian Style village built by the sea near Porthmadog which is at the start of the Lleyn Peninsula. A man who had had a dream and made it come true built it over many years. The scenery through the Vale of Clwyd and Snowdonia as we journeyed west was breathtaking and even though we live in the area we cannot fail to be impressed at the changing seasonal views and vistas.

We parked up in the square in Tremadog, which is just outside Porthmadog and Ned left me on the Wing whilst he stood guard on the corner to make sure that the riders did not miss the turn. As I sat comfortably in the sun watching all around me, a man came out of a shop and, hailing a friend across the square, he got into his van and *reversed* straight into the Wing which he pushed backwards—with me on it! He was about to drive off oblivious to the havoc he had caused when Ned, on seeing what had happened and hearing my shouts, ran up and stopped him driving off. Ned insisted on calling the Police as the man was denying all knowledge of being at fault so Ned tried to get in touch with the Runs leader. Eventually he made contact, one Wing returned, and the outcome was to leave the matter there. Fortunately there was no structural damage.

Our arrival in Portmeirion, the Italianate Village, was delightful. There was a wedding taking place in the hotel and, as we wandered in the gardens below, we saw above us towering over the wall a famous English Goalkeeper who was very pleasant as he obligingly allowed us to take photos. The coastal paths made a lovely walk in the sunshine and the glorious weather made the rides along fabulous roads and the whole day all the more enjoyable.

Birthday Party Surprise.

The other big event of the year was the British International Treffen in Carmarthen which again co-incided with Ned's birthday. It was a special birthday for Ned as he qualified for a bus pass this year! We did not join the main ride-out but went with a few friends to Tenby where our lead rider had no qualms about riding through the pedestrianised part of the town. It was a good 'posing' opportunity which is one thing that Gold Wingers like to do. We parked up and wandered down to the beach where we paddled in the sea and took photos. It was a lovely day and very sunny, which made the lunch of fish and chips taste even better.

Just Us Two

As our Joint Regional Reps had started to have a cocktail party at the Treffen for the region and other friends, I decided to enlist their help to make it into a party for Ned. I organised a cake in my local store for collection in Carmarthen and supplied enough money for extra food and bubbly. The cake was secreted in the boot of another Wing so that Ned would not see it and three lady Wingers dressed up as Bunny Girl waitresses with black shirts & trousers, white bow ties, bunny ears and silver trays. Balloons and bunting around the gazebo completed the scene along of course, with the lethal cocktails concocted by our two intrepid leaders. The Wingers gave Ned a pendant so that he would not forget how old he was. I had also bought sixty candles and he blew them out in one go. On the Sunday we were again Marshalls but this time on the 'Parade of Nations'. This is where as many bikes as possible set off on a planned route through the town. There are Wingers from all over Europe at these International events. Some dress up and all make sure that someone from their country is carrying their national flag. (Each country holds a Treffen, which is organised under the Gold Wing European Federation [GWEF] rules and you could spend a full summer going from one to another if you had the time and money.)

It is quite a sight as music plays and klaxons sound. Locals and visitors line the streets waving and cheering and we graciously acknowledge, with a wave of the hand, this adoration. The local police do a fabulous job in keeping everything moving and, as only they can stop the traffic, they work with the organisers to make sure that we all follow the rules. From Carmarthen, we went on a tour of our scattered family in England and riding eastwards along the breadth of South Wales we rode over the Severn crossing, detoured further into the West Country to see something of North Devon and Cornwall before moving on to Plymouth in the South West and then across to Suffolk.

All in all we travelled the length & breadth of Wales over the summer and saw much of Lancashire and Yorkshire. One Sunday, along with a few others, we rode into Lancashire to Rivington Barn near Bolton in Lancashire. In our younger days this used to be famous for its Saturday night dances with buses laid on from most towns for transport. (Ned did some reminiscing and I hasten to add that this was before he met yours truly and I had never been allowed to taste the delights of these events.) Today it is a Mecca for bikers to meet up and it was crowded with bikes of all shapes and sizes. In the main barn I wandered with a friend around the craft stalls and espied a unique Gold Wing belt buckle. I quickly made my purchase with the intention of hiding it until Christmas. Ned was over the moon with it and he still wears it constantly. This was another beautiful day and the woodland walks were very inviting.

More Diverse Travels of the Way Worn Winger

The epic travels of 2003. Tenerife (again), Ireland re-visited, Cannes/Lake Garda, Italy/ Simplon Pass/Lake Geneva, Switzerland.

The plan this year was to complete the Italy/Switzerland part of the touring schedule which we had dreamt up when we bought the Gold Wing in 1998.

Tenerife.

We started 2003 however, with our usual trip to Tenerife where Ned, having withdrawal symptoms at not being on the Wing, thought that he would pretend. We rented a *scooter* and setting off, we chugged up Mount Tiede with me clinging on to Ned as I perched on the pillion seat. *(Yes, Mary, we are mad but it is fun!)* It was a glorious day and the journey up through pine forests was uneventful on the windy roads. Ned was concerned at the alarming rate in which the fuel gauge dropped.

We stopped for a cooling drink in a mountain village where upon my mobile phone rang. Surprise, surprise, it was one of my learners trying to discuss a point in their learning programme. I quickly explained that I was not in the office, was on leave and would contact on my return. Such dedication! At least I answered! Continuing ever upwards we came to the Cable Car Station and Restaurant where we found a window seat and admired the views of this fairly barren volcanic landscape as it lay in the sunshine. As we had used up quite a lot of petrol on the way up we were on the last drop on the way down. Ned was really worried and calculated that we would probably run out before we reached civilisation. We really were getting desperate and the only bright side was that I suggested that we could always coast downhill. As it was, we found the petrol station in the Orotava Valley just in time. We had stopped to ask a couple of young lads where the nearest fuel stop was and, with sign language, they told us one kilometre. Well, they must have meant one kilometre in a straight drop down the hillside and switchback roads as it was a very, very long one kilometre.

Coming down through the green and leafy Orotava Valley we hit the coast road on the north of the island. It was unexpectedly quite chilly here and we were glad that we had not chosen to stay on this side of the island. We did not linger in Puerto de la Cruz but carried on along the coast where we came upon Garachico, a fishing village on the North West coast. We stopped to look around and get our bearings. We had visited this village before with friends on a previous visit. The signposts indicated that, in order to reach the south we should turn left away from the sea. This took us on a road which rose steeply from the village. It snaked up the mountainside with only a low wall between us and the sheer drop into the sea below. I hoped that we would not miss a corner or we would have tumbled over the wall and down into the sea. The view as I looked down from my perch behind Ned was fantastic! I could see the whole of the coastline with the sea crashing on the rocks below. (In 2007 we were to visit again and reflected how we had made the journey on a little scooter. No we hadn't been mad—just grabbing all the experiences we could while we could.)

The northern coast had been a chilly contrast from the sun on Mount Tiede and reaching the high road, we were glad to turn southwards to ride through the Banana Plantations with glimpses of the coastline glistening below in the sun as we made our way back to our very plush hotel where smart cars populate the garage. The security guard there was very dubious of letting us park up our little scooter. It did not really fit the image of the hotel and clientele. Even when we showed him our room card, he was reluctant to let us in but, when we pointed to our GWOCGB logos on our fleeces, a look of marked respect came into his eyes and he understood. Aahhh! Gold Wing!

Ireland re-visited.

At Easter we went off on the Wing to the west coast of Ireland to see and meet up with family. As Mum was now able to make the journey following Dad passing away, Theresa, who lives on Achill Island, had invited us to bring her and stay saying that she would also have her mother to stay so that these two old friends could meet for the first time and get to know one another. Mum had never visited her roots or her cousin Martha with whom she corresponded over the years as their families grew up. My sister expressed the wish that she wanted to be the one to take Mum to Ireland so we changed our plans and arranged that Mum travelled with my sister in the car. We went on the Gold Wing and stayed with Bridie at the old family home.

County Mayo and the Ballycroy/Achill areas are so very beautiful and the northern coast in this part of Ireland is very wild. Arriving on Good Friday we settled in. Bridie's daughter, a teacher and my second cousin once removed, was home for Easter so it was quite a gathering. In the evening the family went off into the village for a get together. My cousin was dispatched back to bring us to the jollities but we were shy and tired and could not believe that they would really want us there and we opted for bed. We really ought to have made the effort.

On our journey up the coast from Westport we had noticed, on reaching the turning for Achill Island, that the road signs had been changed to give Achill priority. This meant that any unsuspecting tourist was in danger of missing the road to the North West and Ballina. My Celtic roots came to the fore and I later wrote to the local council with a very good case of restoring them. I was successful I believe.

Mum's first meeting with her family was very emotional and tales of the past flew back and forth. They filled in a lot of gaps and it now transpired that there was now some contact with the branch in America. There was another cousin of Mum's age still alive (and in her late eighties). What hardy stock I come from! (On our return I set about contacting my second cousin there and corresponded with her for a while.) We also visited with Mum her father's old home— which was just a couple of miles away— and another cousin, Siobhan, and her husband Martin. Needless to say, this was a very emotional time for them all. On Easter Sunday Mum was able to attend Mass in the church where her parents grew up and were married. We left her to her thoughts as she made her way around the church, examining all the names on the benches and windows as she reflected on the past and her heritage. Bridie looked quite proud as we all sat in the same bench and as she later introduced us to her neighbours.

One day, while Mum and my sister explored, we rode out to Ballina which was further north on the coast. As we rode along the coast we battled with the fierce wind and stopped for a respite to take photos. It was very quiet and on the way back we explored the villages en route. What a wild and wonderful country is this. We strolled back to 'the old house' and tried to imagine what life would have been like, perched on this rocky shore above the sea.

We visited Theresa and Thomas on Achill before we left. They live in such a pretty spot with their garden going right down to a rocky inlet in the seashore. In days gone by I believe it used to be a landing stage where the boat bringing supplies, landed. Mum had been very comfortable there and enjoyed getting to know her namesake. For the return journey home, we decided to travel back down through Galway before crossing Ireland to catch the ferry from the east coast. As it rained heavily the day was a washout and ended with a huge traffic jam near Dublin which caused us to fear that we would miss our sailing. We behaved ourselves and stayed with the traffic but as time began to run out, Ned said that there was only one way to make it to the ferry; so he rode down the white line, overtaking everything and everyone—with caution! These delays did make the journey across Ireland rather tedious but we caught the ferry in time and were soon on home ground with only a two-hour journey from Holyhead to home.

France, Italy and Switzerland.

In between those two trips (Tenerife and Ireland) we heard about the weddings which two of our children planned for around the same time later in the year. Children you ask? They were children no longer. We decided that if we didn't go ahead now as planned we might never do the Italy/Switzerland trip even though our 40th Wedding Anniversary celebrations for the following year had been booked and funds ring-fenced. As usual, I had researched and booked all hotels for the trip via the Internet the previous December.

The beauty of planning this way is that if you have to cancel you do not lose any money if it is far enough in advance. In fact most of the hotels had a twenty-four hour cancellation policy and, others only charged the first night if not cancelled early enough. The Internet search also gave excellent detail and maps about the towns where we planned to stop en route, in Italy and especially the French Riviera and Switzerland, which we had not visited at all before let alone on a Wing. I like to match up the hotels with easy access from the roads and junctions and to make sure that we are not too far out from anywhere and that there is secure parking for Ned's beloved baby. We had heard tales of the roads in Italy but after poring over maps galore thought we would bite the bullet and go—just us two. Much of the fun of the adventure is in the planning.

So, in June 2003 we set off for Folkestone and the Tunnel to head for an overnight stop in Reims. We met in our Reims hotel with friends from North Wales Wings who were on their way home and full of their experiences of their first trip on a 'Wing'. It was nice to have company in the evening and share experiences. As this was a long trip we were fairly loaded up. It was also the summer of the heat wave and was *very hot*. We were glad of our new helmets, with the cool lining.

South of France.

Leaving Reims, we rode on down the Autoroute for many miles and skirting Lyon turned east to cross the Hautes Alpes. These are spectacular and majestic to say the least and I kept very busy filming these valleys with their awe-inspiring snow capped mountains which sparkled in the brilliant sunshine and deep blue sky. As we stopped for petrol in the middle of nowhere, high in the mountains, the old lady on duty eagerly sought out our Euro coins as Ned had produced an Irish one and she had not seen one of those before. (This was the year of the great Euro changeover). She was collecting all the denominations from every country and had a special display folder for them on show outside the shop. She was overjoyed at filling in a few more gaps. After downing our cooling drink whilst drinking in the beauty and breathtaking views below us, we continued on the mountain roads via Grenoble and Digne les Bains to Grasse. This road had some wonderful hairpin bends and I was kept busy filming from my perch on the 'Queen Seat' while I hung on with one hand. It took us south—west of Gap— and wound around the mountains with steep climbs as it followed the contours of the land in never-ending twists and turns. We were now in the Alpes de Haut Provence and, as there was little traffic, we were able to enjoy the wonderful, dramatic mountains as they soared into the sky and the verdant valleys below. Our detailed planning was now paying off as we were able to follow the signposts with little trouble. Reaching Digne-les-Baines we encountered very sharp hairpin bends as the road came back on itself. There were road works here and we took our turn in the queue as we watched large vehicles negotiating the limited space for manoeuvre. The sun was high in the sky and as the temperatures rose we were grateful for our breathable protective clothing. From Digne-les-Baines the road continued over the mountains, becoming more tortuous as it snaked its way towards Grasse. Grasse is a perfume centre and I, ever the romantic, had imagined all the flowers growing in the mountains before being carefully selected to make the perfumes we all pay so much for. This was the Route Napoleon and believed to be very scenic. We were not disappointed. The route was fantastic and we gazed in awe at our surroundings, thinking of the hardships the French soldiers must have suffered as they marched over the mountains in the times of the Napoleonic Wars. I had planned this route into our journey as I had read about it in the weekend travel papers and wanted to experience it.

From Grasse we followed the signs for Cannes where we had a three night stop booked. We had some difficulty in following the map as we could not see the hotel as marked. A very kind young motorcyclist, seeing our indecision, stopped to help and indicating that we follow him, took us round the roundabout and to the hotel entrance. No wonder we could not see it. It was not standing on its own as expected but was part of a big apartment block, such a premium was land here. After checking in, Ned went to put his 'baby' to bed in the underground car park. This was controlled from reception by means of a CCTV camera. As the sensors for the entrance are timed and designed for cars, and Ned lost time working out what he had to do and had to balance the bike on the downward slope, there was a moment of panic as he thought the door was going to come down before he was through. After unpacking, we strolled into the town to find dinner and gaze at the yachts moored up in the harbour. The Cannes Film Festival had just finished but we could still sense the excitement of the whole scene. As arranged we met up with old friends Marc and Mary who take their caravan to Fréjus each year. They collected us from our hotel and took us to Monte Carlo and Monaco for a wonderful day out. On the way they stopped to show us the view along the coast. Driving on the coast road we went through many tunnels and they knew just where to park as they came into Monte Carlo with our first sight of the spectacular Casino in front of us. The first stop was a quick visit into the Casino to be shown the unique features of the 'ladies' as Mary had been instructed to by Marc. I was amazed to see how the toilet seat revolved after a flush to sanitise it. I had never seen anything like it before. Amazing! We strolled around the back of the Casino onto the terrace where Marc soon struck up a conversation with a stranger while we admired our surroundings. Strolling along Mary pointed out the Pink Palace of Monaco on the hill across the bay and, wandering through the gardens in the town we rested in the welcome shade of the trees before eventually coming up into Monaco where we had a leisurely lunch in a shady street just off the courtyard of the Pink Palace (ruinously expensive). After this Marc and Mary took us to see the Cathedral and Princess Grace's resting place behind the altar. My friend & I had never imagined when we were growing up in an industrial Lancashire town that one day we would be 'Ladies who Lunch' in Monaco.

We went back down to Monte Carlo on the 'little train' which was just about to leave (the little train which gives a guided tour). Back in Monte Carlo, Ned was thrilled to actually stand at the tunnel exit on the Grand Prix circuit and walk on part of the course. It was like touching the turf at Wembley! (Now, when he watches the Grand Prix he can visualise where the race is up to and say 'I have been there'.) Settling ourselves outside the café opposite the Casino, we waited in vain for a waiter. This gave us time to ponder on the extravagant prices and we unanimously concluded that 'we would not bother', we would go into Nice and find a bottle of pop in the supermarket. Again, as Marc and Mary knew their surroundings from their annual visits, we were able to park up in a convenient spot and after chancing our lives in the six lanes of traffic each way, Mary & I went to a little supermarket, chanced our lives again when negotiating traffic and sat on the Promenade de Anglais on the sea front to cool down before being taken back to our hotel in Cannes. Marc and Mark had wanted to give us a wonderful day out and it certainly exceeded all expectations. This was another experience to treasure in our memory box of adventures.

With our usual 'what about going to ...?' we decided to ride into Antibes and parked in the newer part by the Marina. As Antibes was new to us we had to try and work out from the Information Board in the town, where was the best part to explore. The old town seemed a way out from where we had parked. Wandering round we spent some time admiring the luxurious boats in the marina and I wondered where all the owners were. There always seemed to be a lot of boats moored up in marinas when I thought they should be out at sea. On the way out we chose a different route and found that the old part of the town had not really been so far away but perhaps too far to walk in the heat. We rode through the old part of the town over the cobbles and around the narrow road with only a low wall between the sea and us. This seems to be getting a bit of a habit with us. Antibes is lovely and the road back to Cannes took us through Juan le Pins and right along the sea front. What a wonderful ride with the breeze blowing off the sea onto our bare legs as we had only helmets and gloves for protection. It was too hot for more and only how the locals dress. These ageing rockers were game for anything!

Onwards to Italy.

The next leg of our journey was to Lake Garda. As we set off for Italy early in the morning, we had a slight mishap as, when Ned set off into the narrow road outside the hotel, the bike (heavily laden and weighing half a ton) flipped over on the kerb and we landed in the large wheelie bins on the pavement. (It was bin-man day.) Ned thought that it must have been oil on the wheel from the underground car park. My head and shoulder hit the ground quite hard but as I lay there, I soon followed strict instruction from Ned to:

'Get up quick, there is liquid running out.'

Dazedly, I did.

I thought of asking for help in the hotel but they could not speak English. Some men came to help Ned lift up the Wing, which was quite a feat and impossible on your own when fully loaded. Ned went off down the street to test the bike for damage. I trudged down the street after Ned and when he was sure the bike was OK, he asked if I was alright and he got out the First Aid Kit as I had hurt my elbow and arm and tenderly dressed the damage. He says that he had his priorities right! How did we manage 40 years!

After some deliberation and gritted teeth as I bit my lip to stop my chin wobbling we climbed aboard—after all we had not seen Switzerland yet—and took in the truly amazing scenery as we rode high above the Italian Riviera coast towards the Alps while I nursed my arm. We had not realised that the road would be so high up above the coast, giving stupendous views of the coastline and the glistening sea below as it wound its way round bends and through tunnels in the ever-rising sun as we made our way around the Gulf of Genoa. At Genoa we turned inland towards Alessandria, Brescia and east to Lake Garda. As this was, again, uncharted territory and we wanted to make our destination as quickly as possible, we kept to the motorways, leaving exploration until after we had settled.

We spent five nights in a lovely air-conditioned hotel on the shores of Lake Garda near Sirmione. The very pleasant gardens went right down to the lakeshore. One day we rode right around the lake, through the many tunnels (we lost count) in the intense heat, wearing only shorts and shirts with helmets and gloves for protection. There are many cutouts in the rock, which give natural light. One flash of sunshine highlighted that a group of bikers had stopped for a comfort break at the side of the mountain road, using the lake for convenience. They did not realise that I caught this on camera as I filmed the entrance to the next tunnel. We stopped at Limone for the obligatory (in North Wales Wings) ice cream and watched the ferry come in to shore. It was too hot to trek into the town but contented ourselves with watching activities on the water. We continued along the western shore to the northern most tip of the lake before turning south to ride down the eastern shore. The scenery here was not as spectacular, being flatter, but it did give us a good view of the west shore and the tunnels we had ridden through. Stopping at Malcaseine we had another ice cream and admired the views as we rested in the sun and marvelled at the ride we had just done. It had been a test of inner strength for Ned as he did not know what would be around the corner; at one point all he had was complete blackness on a blind corner as the tunnel went through rock with no light to shine us on our way. That was quite scary as we could have met a vehicle coming the other way. It is not easy to envisage the actual scale of Lake Garda from the maps, or to image the grandeur of the scenery. With all the lakeside towns, it is like a small county or regional area all of its own. Later, a guest at the hotel was very impressed not only that we had done the whole trip all around the lake at all but that we had done that trip on a bike. Do not they realise that a Gold Wing is a different breed of bike?

We had to curtail our planned journey into the Dolomites, at Trento due to the intense heat at 10:00am. Near Trento we stopped for petrol and Ned sensed that I had gone very quiet and asked what the matter was. Normally I am chatting away down the intercom. I said that I could feel my head and feet swelling in the heat and that if I took off my helmet and boots I would not get them back on. Ned agreed that he felt the same and we decided to return to our hotel. The Alps around us were fantastic with their snow-capped peaks. However, Trento had been the original day out destination until we decided to go further, (you know …'what about?'… as I stuck pins into the map,) and so we were really only back to where we had started. (On our return home we heard about all the mosquitoes at Lake Garda at the Italian Treffen and could sympathise, although we had not seen too many). Thankfully reaching our hotel, we cooled off and relaxed in our air-conditioned room and I rested my arm which was quite painful with all the motion.

Setting of early one morning, we had a lovely day in Verona, using the maps to find our way around. We strolled through the town and through the castle. Finding the amphitheatre we fought our way through the crowds and into the coolness of the surrounding streets. At the house where Juliet was reputed to have lived we saw the famous balcony and all the tourists having a photo taken against her statue. As it was so hot we decided to buy lunch at the supermarket and make our way back the short distance to our hotel and have lunch in the coolness of our air-conditioned room. Due to the heat, we had decided not to re-visit Venice as it would be an uncomfortable ride and quite crowded. We opted however to get our laundry up to date ready for the next leg of the journey. Sirmione, on the southern shore

Just Us Two

of the lake is a lovely town and after we had found a good laundry we wandered round the town in the shade with an ice cream. We discussed the possibility of having a boat ride on the lake but on hearing the price we thought it was extortionate and decided to forgo the treat. With laundry collected, bags packed and the Wing loaded up and secured we were ready for Switzerland and the real journey into the unknown over the Alps. We felt that we had laid good plans and found the information on the Internet reassuring. Until you know differently, you think that it will be all different and barren when in fact, everything is quite normal and a better standard that we have back home.

Over the Alps to Switzerland.

Riding west and taking the route above Lake Maggiore we left Italy and headed towards the Alps using the motorways. Due to the heat we had not lingered for a day exploring the Lakes as planned but had pressed on to find a cool shower in the hotel. We had remembered about buying a ticket for the motorways and at a service station Ned purchased a motorway sticker for the windscreen. It seemed a lot of money for the short time we would be on the motorways but better than chancing a fine.

We stopped for lunch in Domodossola which is a small mountain village in a valley and admired the pretty chalet style buildings before we rode over the Simplon Pass to Brig in Switzerland. This had been one of our 'must do's' and looked forward to the experience. I was surprised at how good the roads were even though they were mountain roads. We were over it almost before we knew and, as it happened, I had to make a quick tape change on the camcorder as we flew over and through the tunnels. Ned was in his element and the cruise control on the bike was so useful as he could take it easy whilst flying along. Here the mountains were majestic but, having come from North Wales, we were not too much in awe. It was though, so beautiful and we reflected how far away from home we were—'just us two'!

Using the map from the Internet, we eventually found our hotel after asking a couple of policeman and using sign language and maps. Even the receptionist was suffering in the intense heat. After a cool shower we wandered through Brig which is very picturesque and we were entranced with the very old-fashioned style railway station and mountain trains. There is a good selection of shops and cafes and we settled down at a pavement one to watch the world go by before taking some film and photos. The following morning, making an early start to beat the heat, we rode out of Brig and through the mountains towards Martigny and north to Lac Leman (Lake Geneva). Travelling now from the east of the lake, we headed round the northern shore and westwards towards Nyon as we rode high above the lake and all the famous towns in the brilliant sunshine.

Casino in Monte Carlo

Childhood friends looking towards Monaco and the Pink Palace

Brig on the Simplon Pass

Just Us Two

Nyon, an old Roman town, is just outside Geneva and our hotel where we were to stay for two nights was right on the lakeside. (Good old Internet.) The manager of the hotel looked down his nose at us as we arrived in our biking gear. I later complimented the receptionist for *his* good attentions and complained about the manager.

The climb on foot up into the town was worth it for the view and the priority was to find some water. Using my schoolgirl French, I brought a smile to the face of the shopkeeper as I made my purchase. The whole area is very beautiful and it was still very hot. One evening we walked back to the hotel to find an elderly couple by the bike after they had dined at the hotel. The lady began to *rock it*. Ned pulled out his bike alarm and I shouted to her to stop. She said she wanted to see how heavy it was. We soon put her right on a few points! We had to continue our trips to the 'cash cow' as Swiss Francs slipped through our fingers even more than Euros. The, by now compulsory, trip on the little train (Le P'tit Train de Nyon) gave us a guided tour of the town and was very informative. It was so hot that even all the flags on the lakeside were drooping and still. We spent a pleasant time in the park near the lakeside and explored the town further. What a delightful find. Nyon was only a dot on the map when I chose it for convenience and consulted the guidebook. Reality was a total and unexpected delightful surprise.

Homeward through cool mountains.

After a few days here we were now ready to head home on the last leg of our journey. We loaded the Wing and, making an early start, we rode west from Nyon on the N90, which would take us north through the Jura Mountains, crossing the France/Swiss border in the mountains before joining the N5 to head towards Morez and Champagnole. The Pine covered Jura Mountains are good biking roads with plenty of switchback bends to challenge the rider and we experienced all of this as we rode. All in a day's work for a Gold Wing! The roads were almost deserted and we had a lovely time in the blessedly cool mountain air as we swooped along through the lush green forests drinking in the fresh mountain air. The chalet houses in the villages gave a feeling that we were not in France but in a ski-ing country.

Heading north-west on the N5 through Poligny we safely reached Dole where we joined the A39 to Dijon from where we would join the more populated major roads. Around Dijon we met with a Gold Winger from Yorkshire Wings at one of the service stations. He was full of his trip through Austria and Switzerland. Whenever we stop and see a Gold Wing we always have a chat even if it is in sign language as the men discuss the bikes. We spent our last night in our Reims hotel, consuming many litres of water, before completing the last long leg of four hundred and fifty miles to home to Wales via Calais. I followed my usual practice on reaching British soil; I placed my trust in Ned and went to sleep. The Way Worn Winger was well and truly, way worn!

We have come to realise that we are not getting any younger and perhaps this length of leg to travel—four hundred and fifty miles—is perhaps a bit too much for us now. We have seen most of what we set out to do and the plan now is to do a shorter trip to a base and explore an area more or do the trips over more weeks. Now what was Ned saying about Central Brittany? ... Northern Spain? .... He is even trying to talk himself into braving the ocean waves and using the Plymouth-Roscoff ferry as you will see ...

Changing Lives

A Transformation from Bike to Trike

This year, although a hectic one, was a quiet one on the Winging front. This was due in part to Ned's little health blip on our 40th Wedding Anniversary in 2004 but at least he was able to get back on his bike, (he and his trusty steed are welded at the hip!).

The best laid plans ... When our lives turned upside down.

We had decided not to go out for a meal on our actual anniversary so I put a nice meal of steak, mushrooms, onions etc in the oven to cook slowly. At lunchtime I got a call from Ned to collect him from work as he did not feel well. This was serious! He had been fighting something off for days but would not stay at home, even though he felt he would fall down if he tried to run down the hallway. I dashed off, in between appointments, to collect him and he went off to the see the doctor later in the day as he refused to call him out. Oh! The stubbornness of men!

As I took Ned off to the emergency department at the hospital he said how good the steak smelled and was looking forward to a quiet meal 'a deux'. However our lovely meal burnt to a cinder as the hospital admitted Ned to the Cardiac Ward; his anniversary meal became a thing of the past as the only food in the ward kitchen at that time in the evening was a Tuna sandwich on white bread. Fish is the last thing he would choose to eat so, in desperation as he should not go too long without food, I dashed to the hospital shop which had just closed. They kindly let me in to have a look behind the counter at what Ned could eat, bearing in mind that he couldn't have sugar. The doctors later came round and on hearing about our planned celebrations said that they would do what they could but wanted to concentrate on getting him to forty-one year's married. Seriously though, he is not his usual perky self and is on a management programme to keep him ticking over. After a few days having tests under the supervision of the Cardiologist, the doctors let him out on the Friday and he was able to greet our guests at the Beaufort Park Hotel, albeit sitting down. He managed to walk across the floor to me, for the toast after I had made my speech—where I heaped glowing praise on him for his constant support and encouragement in enabling me to do what I was capable of in life—and for part of the first dance. He looked well, as he always has done, in spite of almost collapsing as he went upstairs in the hotel for the camcorder and found it was too much. All our guests had a good time and once again we thank everyone for making the celebrations everything we wished. We were not to know that he would never work again as the condition was serious.

Back in the Saddle.

It is now July 2005 and Ned has collected his 'baby', which has recovered after major surgery. Many of North Wales Wingers may have thought that the Way Worn Winger was too 'way worn' to continue riding but, not so. During the last three months both Ned and his beloved Wing have been traumatised. Not to mention Rosie who now can't afford any more new shoes!

Early in 2005, reluctantly realising that he would have to bow to the obvious and change his mode of riding he reached agreement with 'her indoors'. Ned began to search the Web (yes, Ned!). He found a site in Minnesota USA who provided landing gear which is the equivalent of putting stabilisers on a child's bicycle. Rosie, being reluctant to buy 'blind', thought that this warranted a site visit, just to make sure they were what Ned really wanted and had even sorted out flight times. Ned then decided against landing gear as a solution to his problem and gave various reasons but Rosie maintains that the real reason was because she wanted to go to America to inspect before buying. A big frown had appeared on someone's head! Ned was reluctant to spend a fortune on giving his baby an extra wheel, mainly as he did not have a fortune. He just wanted to continue riding. The alternative was to confine touring to the lovely Welsh countryside using their free bus passes issued to over 60's courtesy of the local Council. Not an option either was ready for. Ned found various sites for solutions and many thanks go to those North Wales Wingers who e-mailed suggestions.

As Ned is forever nosy and can't resist getting his hands dirty, he had taken off the panniers to have a look at what work would have to be done if he went down the 'triking' route. It was not a pretty sight. Ned had found a trike firm in Devon who converted many different types of bikes but had never done a Gold Wing before. Other firms had cornered the market for this but Ned found them too expensive. After many telephone calls, the firm agreed to use our bike as a prototype and, subject to price and Ned being happy with workmanship, we decided to go down this route.

Ned and Rosie set off for Devon in convoy at Easter. Ned was on the Wing and Rosie drove the car for the return journey. It was a bit nerve wracking on the drive down as Rosie kept watching out to see that Ned was OK and not too tired. It was his first long ride in a long time. It was also an opportunity to see family in Plymouth. The plan was, to be prepared to leave the Wing subject to final agreement on terms etc. As a metal expert and craftsman, Ned was happy with the workmanship of the trikes on display and he put himself and his (their) Wing in the capable hands of the experts. The discussions and ideas had moved on since the initial discussions, from the standard trike conversion and how to 'fill the gap' between the wheels, progressing to a more standard Gold Wing Trike look. This was a great relief as they did not want to be thrown out of the Club for not having a proper job and anyway, what about luggage? With a team of craftsmen a new model was born, as Ned's bike was a prototype. The trike firm would do the work needed to convert from two wheels to three and a fibreglass expert would work with them on the bodywork. Ned made many phone calls regarding progress but in the main, was very patient even though he was 'champing at the bit' and was dying to get his hands on it. He would have loved to have been the one holding the screwdriver etc. …

Eight weeks passed and—no bike. Tragedy! The planned trip to Keltic Wings in Scotland was in the balance. We had met the Keltic Wings Rep. at the AGM in 2004. He had captivated us with the tales of Stirling and the proximity of the Wing Ding site to the town. It seemed ideal and this area was the basis of lots of historical novels. Our plans were well and truly scuppered at the last minute, when the accommodation cancelled out due to a plumbing problem. Although we booked an alternative hotel, it was out of town, weather was bad and forecasts worse. Tenerife beckoned as the weather in February had not been as good as usual and we needed some sun in June—not the forecasted snow in Scotland—but that is another story and it took Ned's mind of his baby's recovery after surgery. Sorry Keltic, perhaps another time.

After many discussions, the trike team had made and modified the mould for the prototype. The trike firm was really into this and their enthusiasm new no bounds. This was something different to the firm's normal line of conversion and they wanted to make sure it was just right. They did the entire paperwork changeover for us which took the hassle out of the 'official' side of things. They sent us some photos of work in progress as Ned, after ten weeks, had bitten his fingers and nails down to his knuckles.

'It looks all right,' he said.

That was an understatement. Apart from limited boot space it was more than all right. As this was a new venture and a deviation from normal conversions, the firm requested feedback from Wingers. This is version 'Numero Uno'. Modifications and perfection are the order of the day. Evidently some of the delay had been due to people stopping for a look as the Wing went from workshop to workshop and MOT etc. They couldn't get a thing done!

One glorious weekend at the end of June, Ned could hardly contain his excitement. D-Day had arrived and we set off for Devon so that Ned could bring his baby home again to Wales. After stopping at Worle, Weston Super Mare for a bite to eat in a lovely olde worlde pub we carried on to Tiverton. As the trip had been arranged at short notice, all the hotels near Exeter were full and Rosie thought anyway that two hundred miles was far enough to travel in one leg. This was also an opportunity to see children over the weekend. Ned and Rosie arrived at the appointed hour the following morning and oh! What a disappointment. Where is my baby? Ned's disappointment was palpable and he thought the journey had been for nothing. Due to other's working patterns and the last bit of paint not being dry, there was a slight delay. They had had mushroom panels painted on the front of the mudguards to match the rest of the bike.

Emerging from the chrysalis. 'He saw his baby, sat astride and smiled.'

At last, Saturday dawned and after spending the previous day in Plymouth with family we said our good-byes and started out northwards to Oakhampton. As we turned in, there it was. Ned saw his baby—looked—pulled his keys from his pocket—sat astride and fired up. What a lovely satisfied smile on his face as he took her for a turn around the apron in front of the workshop to get a feel of how she handled. Of course he had to get down on the ground to have a look underneath at the engineering side of things.

On the way back to the hotel Rosie had a little weep at the passing of an era but, is this start of something new? The following day, she drove ahead and from a distance on the motorway, Rosie thought that there was an eagle landing in the distance. The Wing looked for all the world like a nose and two wings with landing wheels. The spotlight at the front and lights on the mudguards gave that illusion …

Ned had the Wing just before his birthday way back in,'98, a CB Radio for his 60th and now a Trike just before his next birthday! How much more lucky can a man get? Apart from having an understanding wife that is! A pre-requisite for a Winger!

From This

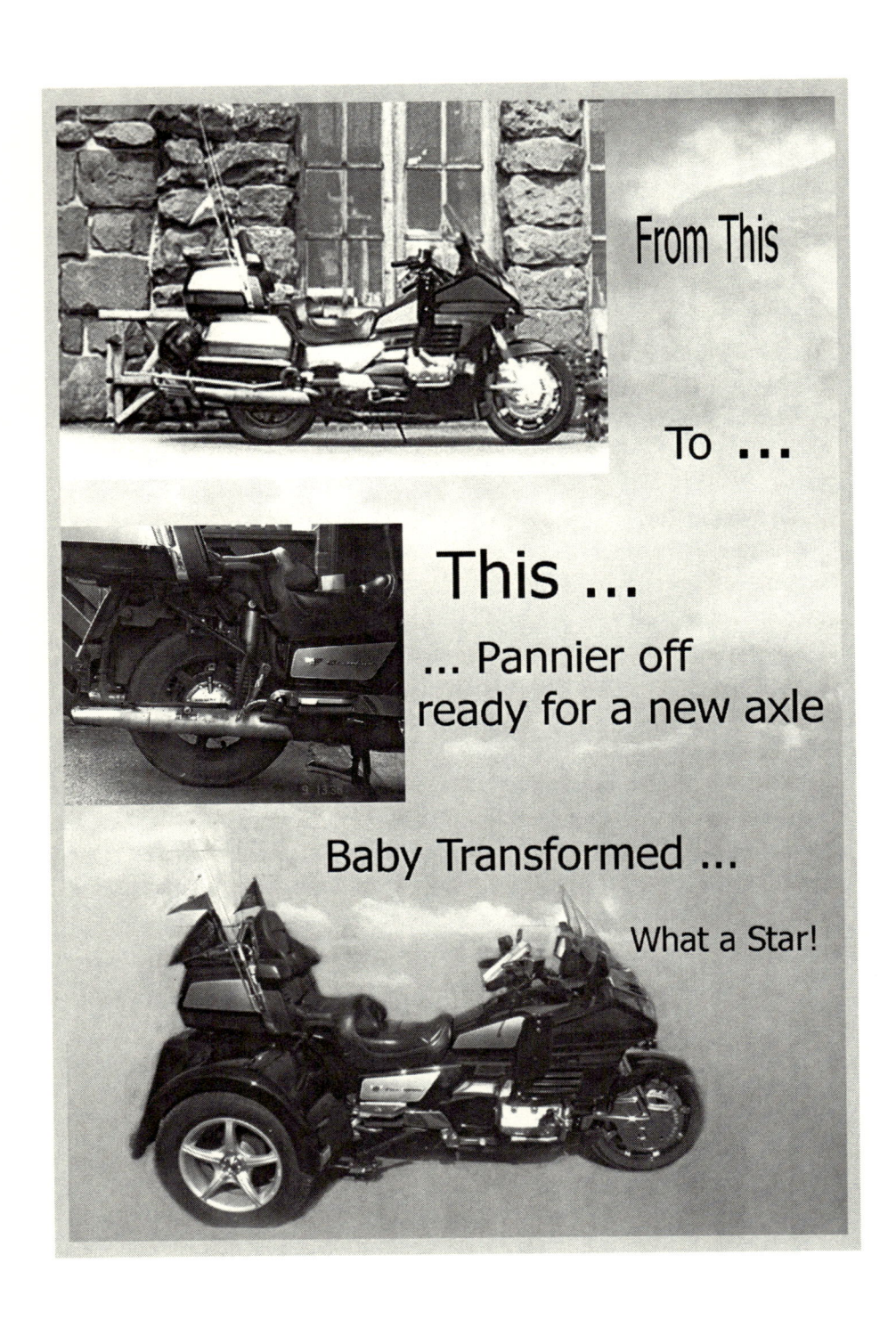

To ...

This ...

... Pannier off ready for a new axle

Baby Transformed ...

What a Star!

From Bike to Trike. The sequel.
As detailed, Ned had reluctantly decided to add an extra wheel to his beloved baby in 2005. Subsequently, there were modifications to the boot and suspension. The result was an even more comfortable ride than previously on two wheels when going over bumps, as testified by 'her who sits on the back and goes to sleep!

The addition of a luggage carrier and tailored bag over each wheel arch, which matched the trunk carrier and bag, completed the outfit and gave all the luggage space needed to counteract the loss of the panniers. In fact, with the addition of a boot, we had actually gained space. All Ned's baby needed now was some decoration on the back to brighten up the expanse of black but this was to be negotiated—no rush. Yes dear reader, there was no rush as it eventually took nearly three years before Ned would come to an agreement as we both moved to the middle road from our individual viewpoints.

Baby in the balance.
The winter of 2005-2006 was very bad here in Wales and the baby stayed cosseted under cover due to salt on the roads. The summer of 2006 was *very, very hot* and, due to memories of the heat in Italy in 2003 plus extreme work commitments; 'her who sits on the back' did not venture far but found it a very comfortable ride when she did. Ned, meanwhile, eventually admitted that he was finding the steering a little hard on short journeys. This was in part, due to a reduction in upper body stamina and the Wing being a very heavy and robust beast. You must remember that when adding another wheel, the whole dynamics of steering changes as you do not 'lean over' on corners but physically drive round and turn.

He had been looking at the new Piaggio three-wheeler with two wheels at the front and one rear wheel. Evidently it would still be OK for touring and there was, he said, decent luggage space. Talk about being in cloud-cuckoo land! Was 'her who sits on the back' going to be thrilled at having to relinquish a comfortable seat for a *perch*? Especially as it was 'her who sits on the back' who had decreed in the first place, way back in 1998 after owning a Pan European for two months, that the Goldwing she had beheld and stood transfixed before in the showroom was the only thing if touring was on the agenda. The first chapter of this story (and those GWOCGB members who read the Wing Span articles will remember our article published in December 2000) detailed how Ned thought he had died and gone to heaven at this announcement. Subsequent chapters and articles have detailed our journeys. How *could* he think of downsizing? He must be mad; perhaps it was another mid life crisis? It must be serious. It was not to be borne.

Here followed a concentrated attempt at soft selling the idea to 'her who sits on the back'. The shop in Chester would be having the new Piaggio in after Christmas. They were a good price etc.etc. We paid a visit to the Bike Show at the National Exhibition Centre in Birmingham in November 2006. Ned was keen to seek out the new 3-wheeler but he was in for a disappointment as there were no Italian bikes there to speak of. We did see on one stand a conversion which allowed the rider to ride on in a wheel chair and still give the effect of riding a bike. I thought that seeing that side of life had put things into perspective. For someone who had always had bikes, it was hard. At the annual Gold Wing service, our service engineer mentioned an expensive modification but urged Ned to persevere as he was sure that Ned would be converted to the different riding experience and all seemed well. What a false sense of security I was in ...

Reprieve for the baby.

We had a friendly visit over Christmas 2006 from our good friend and Regional Rep. and the conversation suddenly turned to Ned announcing that he had been thinking of changing to the bike with two wheels at the front and one rear wheel. I more or less said 'enough!' Our friend was astounded at Ned's announcement and talked about 'leading links' and to try out a trike which had them fitted. He is a man of action and that evening sent us a Web link for a firm in California who supplied EZ-Steer which effectively gave the effect of power steering and increased the stock rake angle by approximately 4.5°.

Following this I did some undercover work by expressing my concerns to another Winger and asked if his wife would get on the back of one of those with two wheels at the front and one wheel at the back. He gave a shake of the head and a long 'Noooooooooo'. Another Winger friend commented on what modifications other bikes had. So, after sourcing the information given by our friend for supply direct or via the UK dealer and after speaking to the USA dealer direct for Gold Wing prices and shipping costs to the UK, we purchased by phone one Monday evening early in January 2007 and received the parts by Wednesday morning. With the help of our friend who followed in his car for the journey back, Ned took the trike one very snowy winter's day to our specialist service engineer—the only person he would allow near his beloved 'baby'—who quickly fitted the new extension to the steering.

On the return visit to collect the trike, Rosie drove ahead. As he pulled into the drive at home behind her, she asked Ned with baited breath how it was and had it worked. He gave an unmistakable nod of the head. The trike really did give the feel of power steering now. 'He who must be obeyed' had a smile on his face again and 'her who sits on the back' breathed a sigh of relief. She dreamed that she would soon be back in business with the camcorder as they flew over the Millau Viaduct in France …

Final thoughts on the conversion.
Overall, suffice to say that we were puzzled as to why we had not heard or read, of a whisper of the 'drag' effect when converting to three wheels. We had not read of any technical information anywhere that it even *is* an issue; let alone how to solve the problem.

Possibly there is information on the Internet but Ned is not a Web browser and the point is that the problem did not anywhere, in all his varied conversations, come into the equation. Once we did broach the subject, our friends in North Wales Wings bent over backwards to supply what information they could. Thank you one and all. So, for those of you who are thinking of triking, perhaps through the well-advertised suppliers or via a more independent alternative route, there is an extra 'bit', which needs to be costed in to the conversion, and there *are* choices. For triking we went down the independent route on grounds of cost, tailored to fit and value for money and it could be that lighter bikes do not have the same difference in steering and therefore the subject did not seem important. We hope that you have found our tale of trauma interesting and informative and that it is of help to others who are thinking of modifications.

The future.

In the meantime we had vaguely planned a trip to France for September 2007 as by this time all the work on the house would be done and grandchild number four born and bonded with. Ned wanted to go to Carcassonne again, I wanted to go over the Millau Viaduct, and we would finish off with a family visit in Brittany. Now that Ned was happy with his 'baby' it all seemed possible even though we were not sure if Ned would be fit to travel when the time came. Ned, although not a good traveller, said that he would chance a sailing from Portsmouth to Cherbourg in Northern France on a fast ferry. Before we could book we received a special offer leaflet from Norfolk Line, over the Christmas period, about some new sailings from Dover to Dunkerque. They had built three new ships and catered for cargo, freight and motorist only, sailing the Calais-Dunkerque route. For £19 one way (out of season) or £29 one way (in season) with a £5 supplement for weekend crossings, it was £58 in all for us for bookings made up to the end of January 2007 and with sailings up to twenty-four hours a day, we quickly re-planned and re-costed the trip.

Although sailing from Dover added miles and one overnight stop to the previous plan, it was much cheaper. Although not certain that it was a good idea and thinking of all the 'what ifs' we bit the bullet and booked the trike on to the ferry and then booked all the hotels. (We thought that, if needed at the last minute we could change for the car and even cancel if we had to as we did not pay for hotels in advance). There was no extra charge for car-trike over motorbike as it appears that the ferry company cater for everyone as a motorist. The software on the Web site adjusts the length of vehicle automatically to suit the class of vehicle being booked on. The standard price seemed the usual hefty fee though so we were glad to get a good deal. Watch this space ...

Next stop, en Francais!

Business as Usual

On our way at last! Just Us Two!

It has been a long journey in more ways than one since our trip in 2003 to Cannes in the South of France, Lake Garda in Italy, Brig on the Simplon Pass and Nyon on Lac Leman in Switzerland.

Re-cap.

After finally realising in late 2005 that even two wheels was no longer an option, we had set in motion the process of triking the bike. As it was a prototype, the suspension and steering had needed various refinements. In January 2007, even before we fitted EZ-steer from the USA, we decided to 'bite the bullet' and book what we felt could be our last long touring trip. It was not certain for many months, that we would actually be able to go due to possible health treatments etc. for Ned but it was something to plan and focus on. Someone said to me after our North Wales Wing Ding 2000 that 'I had to realise that a Gold Wing is not just a bike but a passion'. I had replied that 'it is not my passion; I just go along with it'. They say that you don't value something until you are in danger of losing it and it is now apparent to me, after being in danger of losing the relaxing freedom and comfort of Gold Wing travel and exploration and having 'negotiated' to keep it, that I have become more passionate about the uniqueness of Gold Wings in general and Ned's 'baby' in particular which had become part of the family.

As usual, we made extensive preparations. It is all in the planning. Ned wanted to go to Carcassonne again and I wanted to go over the

Millau Viaduct. I had also wanted to join the Annual Diocesan trip to Lourdes but Ned did not at this time and I would not leave him. Therefore we added a two-night stay in Lourdes in the foothills of the Pyrénées to our return trip, stopping off in La Rochelle on the west coast before visiting family in Bretagne. I did the usual research into maps, routes, A.A. AutoRoute for mileage plus hotels etc. and, after much discussion, costing the trip and making bookings with the Ibis Central Reservations Service, plans were in place. This initial planning is very detailed, essential to a smooth trip and all part of the fun. We do not have a Sat. Nav. for directions as Ned says he has one sitting behind him on the Wing. Although we agree that they have their uses, we cannot understand how some people can rely on them utterly and not have even a picture of the route in their minds or a map for reference. After poring over a map, I keep bringing up a picture of the route in my mind's eye. All part of the fun we say. We had decided to book hotels through Ibis, which is part of the Accor Group, as they are easily accessible. Helpfully, the hotel guide gives little maps and directions from various points which allow one to decide if you want a hotel on the outskirts of a town or more central to allow for some exploring. Another factor is the cancellation arrangements—which are very accommodating to say the least—so that even if we had to cancel any of the rooms at the last minute we would not lose out. In addition, the other factor for choosing Ibis (or indeed any similar type of hotel/motel) is that you can book an easy access room whether it is ground floor or near to a lift. Thus we are able to avoid stairs and the vexed question of luggage porterage and carrying bags. I was a little concerned about the weight and size of the luggage bag which fits into the trunk bag and, despite assurances, I remained unconvinced that lifting it out would not be a problem. I subsequently insisted that we take my little collapsible trolley so that I could use that for trundling the bags back and to. In addition, we decided that we would pack our first few days of overnight changes into the luggage bag which fitted on the trunk rack, just taking out of the large trunk bag what we needed, as we needed it, if at all. Obviously packing had to be planned carefully and we reverted to what we did when we went to Italy on a three to four centre holiday all those years ago and 'packed into days' etc. As I wrote earlier, the initial plan was to take the ferry

Just Us Two

to Cherbourg as Ned said he would try the fast ferry and we costed this into the budget but changed this plan to a sailing from Dover to Dunkerque. Although we booked the trike on as a car, there was no difference in price to a bike; it was just a case of calculating overall capacity etc. There were however no refunds in the case of cancellation but as you have an insurance cancellation excess, we thought that we would not be out of pocket if we had to cancel. Sailings were every two hours and took one hour and forty-five minutes; they did not cater for coaches and foot passengers which enhanced comfort. The change actually added another overnight stop each way onto the trip and more miles but we decided to go with it as the crossing was shorter. Perhaps we should have gone our usual route in the tunnel after all but it is quite expensive considering.

In August, after various tests indicated that the proposed additional treatment, being too risk was not a viable proposition, we decided that we had to 'just get on with it'. We were well and truly 'back in business'. Our trip was on and we were all set to get preparations under way for our September 1st departure. During the intervening weeks there was much preparation. Ned with the bike—polishing, cleaning wheels etc.—Rosie buying town centre maps and new clothing. Sizing was a traumatic experience, as any curvy lady of a certain age will testify; getting clothing that fits in the right places can be a trial. Fortunately, there is now a big demand for clothing made to a woman's shape so that we now do not have to try to mould our shape to that of a man's jacket/trouser design. Once I had settled on a pair of trousers that fit in all the right places and looked fashionable and stylish, I looked again at jackets and jazzy summer gloves. Oh, the jacket *is* smart with a good cut and lots of detail in the shape of zips, Velcro, leather touches and trims. The gloves have vents on each finger and shaped 'nails' at the tips (perhaps I should paint them pink?!). There is also a shaped knuckle protector (watch out Ned) and a lilac contrast. Just the ticket! After the entire 'fittings' trauma of the last few months, I deserved all these new riding feathers.

Finally, the great day dawned. Ned set the alarm for an early start. At our second stop at the Clackett Lane Services on the London M25 southbound; I was investigating the insides of my jacket. (It had been stashed it away in the cupboard after the recent purchase and I had not looked at it in detail.)

'Oh look! I have a pocket for a mobile phone in the lining!' I said.

'Do you know?' Ned said, 'I have not put the mobile phone in the bike!'

After some moments of consternation, we decided to ring family to alert them. Thankfully, we had left a list of hotel stops and telephone numbers. We decided that, as before the advent of mobile phones we all managed without, we would manage now as the hotels had phones in the room. It might be a bit of a problem though if we were stuck on a mountain or remote road but we pushed these negative thoughts firmly to the back of our minds. This truly was getting away from it all and a lesson in how much we had come to rely on the availability of instant access. A fleeting thought was to bin it altogether!

Dover to Rodez via Boulogne, Chartres and Limoges.

We arrived early at Dover and were in time for an earlier 2:00pm crossing. We were allowed on with no administration charge for change of sailing time (another bonus), and settled ourselves in the Veranda Lounge as the ship pulled away. It is only as you leave the harbour that the beauty and significance of the White Cliffs are apparent. The sea was— thankfully for Ned—like a millpond and the crossing smooth.

Disembarking was easy and we arrived at our Boulogne hotel, thankfully not too late. The extra maps which I had pulled of the Internet for all the hotel locations were a useful addition to the Hotel Guide. The earlier crossing was a blessing as we had to put our clocks forward by one hour. It had been an early start, a long ride and we were both tired and ready for a shower and dinner. The following morning was a Sunday and our next leg was south to Chartres. It was chilly with grey skies and, as we rode through Boulogne to find the Auto Route out of town, the church bells were ringing, blending their tune with the early Sunday morning atmosphere as the sun peeped through the clouds. The size of the town surprised me.

We had ridden through on our first Gold Wing trip to France eight years before but had not realised the size of it. We rode past

Just Us Two

the Cathedral and from the A16 as the sun rose, we could see how it dominated the town. It was, surprisingly, situated within fortified walls, indicating how the town would have been—in times gone by— a bastion to invaders. Riding along the A16 and A28 we travelled via Abbeville, Neufchatel-en-Bray. Joining the A13 at Rouen we travelled to J19 to pick up the N154 to Evreux, before we came to Dreux and then Chartres. The day had been cold and wet with nothing much to see let alone film and, after a testing year, I was very tired. I was so tired that I dozed off from time to time as Ned made his way south. The only bonus today was that, being Sunday, heavy lorries were not allowed on the motorways. We checked in to our hotel and slept! I had planned the distances so that we could relax and explore each town before the day was out. As it was, after a three hour sleep there was only time for dinner as we looked out despondently at the weather.

The following morning, as we checked the route out of town, we espied a Gold Wing in the Car Park in the square near the hotel. It was a beautiful black and burgundy one and very tasteful with the seat back-rest having black in the centre and burgundy on the outside. It was a USA specification and Ned had not heard of one before. (He knows his bikes!) He took a photo, which was a casualty in a later 'happening' as will be narrated later. Monday dawned and today's leg was to Limoges. I had wanted to see the town (and the area) as this is where the famous Limoges porcelain is made. What a letdown! It was a long, long road. It was a very straight road but a long one as far as the eye could see and it was: cold, wet, windy, and soul destroying. We continued from Chartres along the N154 /A10 to by-pass Orleans and then travelled along the A71 (Vierzon), A20 Autoroute L'Occitane (and I thought that L'Occitane was a perfume brand!), via Chateauroux to Limoges. The lie of the land was flat fields as far as the eye could see and uninteresting. I did not bother with the camcorder as there was nothing to see in the wet and mist. I snoozed along the way, contrary to what Ned had expected as he had said that this would not be possible on a trike due to the difference in handling etc. I proved him wrong and …I did not fall off! We did not really stop for lunch as we had had a relatively late start (10:00am). In the event, snacking was a mistake as by the time we had checked in, Ned was feeling quite low and hungry. Not good for a diabetic. Nearer to

Limoges, it warmed slightly and I perked up but Ned had by now put in his jacket liner—September 3rd and like winter!

Using the Ibis map and those from the Internet I was able to direct Ned through the city to our hotel in the centre. Limoges was much bigger than I had imagined. Tall imposing buildings, dirty from exhaust fumes and two thousand years of dirt, rose high into the sky on narrow streets. (We were in the Centre Ville). We were able to unload outside the hotel and they had a luggage trolley but parking was confusing to say the least as the hotel had advertised garage parking but the receptionist directed Ned to the paying one up the street while I unpacked.

The Car Park Saga.

After we had changed, we strolled out so that Ned could look at the way out for the morning and I wanted to see if the Wing was safe. We were not happy with the open-air overnight parking and went back to the hotel to enquire about hotel parking as advertised. All to no avail,

'Impossible,' 'full,' the receptionist brushed us off with.

'Is the open air one safe?' we enquired.

A shrug of the shoulders was the reply. No amount of pleading that it was a very expensive bike, helped

'We are not happy!' we stated, bearing in mind that Accor have a 100% satisfaction pledge.

The receptionist produced a town plan and pointed to an underground car park. Off we went, and after a reccae of the road system, Ned sussed the way out of the open-air car park and I paid the €0.60 cent fee. We rode around to the underground one and, as we took the ticket at the entrance barrier, the attendant, who was sweeping up at the end of the day, stopped us.

'*No Moto!*' she cried waving her arms.

We gesticulated that it was not a bike.

'No Moto,' she kept saying.

We could not understand each other and she directed us down the ramp as we were obstructing others. What a pantomime this was and we were desperate as we could not just turn around and wanted safe parking. We assured her, using sign language and my limited French, that we would pay the car fee but still she came back with 'crossed arms sliced open' saying '*No Moto*' and jabbered away in

French. Well it was her native language and we were in France after all! In exasperation, she contacted her boss on her mobile phone and put us on. I attempted to explain in a mixture of broken French and English that it was:

'Not un Moto, très wheels, l'auto. Stay un nuit. Tomorrow, Carcassonne, Lourdes, La Rochelle'.

His reply was unintelligible. I could not understand. I repeated desperately:

'No Moto, a GoldWing, l' auto—stay un nuit a Ibis Hotel'.

His manner changed and perked up. I pleaded with him!

'No authority!' he said.

I handed the phone back to the attendant and in total defeat, dropped my head on Ned's shoulder. Out of the corner of my eye I could see a movement in the 'help' office at the end. All at once the attendant said:

'OK. Stay.'

Oh the relief! It was indescribable as we don't know what we would have done if we had had to leave. We would have worried all night, especially as the receptionist did not seem confident of our 'baby's safety in an open air car park. Ned went to the next level and put his baby to bed. I shook the girl's hand, showed her our Ibis room card as proof of what I had said to the attendant and kissed her as she directed us out to our hotel. The word 'Ibis' seemed to work wonders. They are part of the Accor Group, as I have already said, and very big in France. Check in is simple and cancellation allowed to 7:00pm with no charge. Perhaps we should have arranged parking at the hotel in advance. We were not to know it was limited.

Feeling happier and more relaxed, we went for a gentle stroll round to stretch our legs and re-lived the experience over a drink. I had a beer called Desperado, with no idea of what it was, as I had felt desperate and it suited my mood. It was flavoured with Tequila! Uuughh! Say no more. After exploring a little we went back to the Brasserie for eats but they did not serve until 7:00pm so we went to the one on the corner of the square and had a lovely 'boef dish (with legumes)' marinated in cider. The weather had improved by now and an early night was called for as we had planned an early start the following morning before the city got busy with traffic. Ned had thought this morning that the alarm clock was broken and reflected that with forgetting the mobile and a broken alarm, we were destined to really get away from it all. Actually, he just had not heard the buzzer. Tongue-in-cheek, I could not resist the observation that the alarm on the mobile was quite efficient but he had forgotten it!

To Rodez.
Tuesday morning dawned, with good weather promised for the day and we were up bright and early to bring the trike round from the car park to load up. We had a mild panic as I thought I had thrown away the ticket in error. (The open-air car park was the same firm). I had not! As we set off at 8:40am, the sun was shining and the sky was blue. I was a happy bunny again as I took film along the way. At Brive la Gaillarde we left the A20 and picking up the N140 we rode through this most beautiful part of France. The scenery was more interesting now and at times we were quite high up as we continued south to Rodez via Figeac and the Lot Valley.

Figeac is a delightful, pretty, medieval town on the River Célé and was well worth the stop. We had happened upon it by chance as I had only pinpointed Rodez as our overnight stop and that was very much a shot in the dark as we had never heard of it before. We had lunch in an upstairs Terrace Restaurant overlooking the river. As is practice in many parts of France, 12:00 noon to 2:00pm is devoted to eating an enormous meal and everywhere closes. In fact they do not serve until 12:00 noon. Sadly, we could not manage all that was on the menu. It was quiet of tourists as it was either at the end, or out of season and it was nicer that way. We were glad of Ned's Blue Badge to park just a few feet away as the car parks were on the edge of town, quite a walk away and were full. There are lots of campsites for Caravans and Motor Homes in the area. Our route had taken us through the Vallée de Lot and after Figeac into the Vallée de Averyon through the most beautiful and contrasting countryside on good roads. Later, as we entered Rodez, we could see how the Cathedral dominated the town; as is the case with all the towns we have seen on this trip—Boulogne, Chartres and Limoges to name a few. We followed the signs, as instructed, for the Centre Ville. This took us in front of the Cathedral, on cobbles! As we bounced along I was thankful for three wheels but Ned said it was better on two wheels. I assured him that I was having a more comfortable ride (even over bumps) than ever I did on two wheels and that I had been mainly comfortable (except for big bumps). As we rounded the Cathedral and the sharp bend down to the hotel, I had a glimpse of a most fantastic view of the valley which spread out below. I had not realised that the town was so high up. When choosing the route it had been guesswork, looking at the terrain on maps and then finding hotels. Both Figeac and Rodez were, for different reasons, an utter delightful surprise. They more than made up for the disappointment and frustrations of Limoges. Monday had been a seriously low point but today we were on the up and hoped it would stay that way.

The Ibis Hotel in Rodez is new and more to standard than Limoges had been. After a shower, 'glamming up' and parking, we set off to explore the town and for Ned to see the fantastic view over the valley and take some photos. As the camcorder battery was low, filming was out. (Wait for the ensuing calamity with the photos …). Over dinner we reflected on the next stage of our journey. Tomorrow would bring the Millau experience on the Viaduct. We had ridden on the tortuous road down the valley into the congested town in 2000 after we had been to Andorra and had heard a lot about this magnificent construction high across the Tarn Valley. We thought a photo on the bridge itself would be good. We had charged the camcorder up again and Ned's new camera has lots of space on the card. After Millau we would be spending three nights in Carcassonne. What bliss!!

The Carcassonne Adventure.
Wednesday dawned with a happy rising sun. We would have liked to have spent longer in Rodez. The town was a total delightful surprise and chosen as a marking point (mileage) for the journey to Carcassonne. There are flights from Stanstead Airport to Rodez so, perhaps one day, we will come again. Leaving Rodez on the N88 we travelled eastwards via the D911 to the A75. Approaching Millau we could see the huge imposing structure—like sails pointing high in the sky—in the distance. Ned could not fathom how we were to go onto the bridge from where we were. The road wound around and swept majestically across the Tarn valley and we were on the viaduct almost before we knew it. We had stopped earlier for Ned to set me

up with his camera as we wanted a picture of us crossing, not only for us but also for our North Wales Wings Rep. Ned of course, being an engineer, wanted pictures of the structure. So, with camera around my right wrist and anchored in the Velcro of my jacket sleeve fastening, I held it in my left hand. I pushed 'on' and focussed for pictures. In my right hand I pointed the camcorder and pushed 'record'. So—there I was—click, click, check camcorder, OK.

'Get those structures,' Ned instructed.

The camcorder had to take potluck but I got some good shots of the back of Ned and the front of the bike and, of course, the bridge supports, as we flew over the bridge. It was over all too soon …and, importantly, I did not fall off. At Junction 47 we picked up the D999 (signposted to St Serin-sur-Rance/Albi/St. Affrique), and turned westwards then south to travel via St.Affrique to Carcassonne.

At St. Affrique we stopped to stretch our legs. Again, as is the custom in France, they do not take the lunch hour of 12:00 noon to 2:00pm into account for car parking purposes and our one-hour stretched to three hours. We decided to have a drink and find lunch. St. Affrique is only a dot on the map but in truth it is a lovely country village and a complete surprise as we had thought that there would be nothing much there. We had a cooling drink in a bar and moved away to dodge cigarette smoke and big dogs. The dog's owner (two dogs of the same breed) shook hands with the animal and then picked up his freshly bought bread which was wrapped only in a serviette! Strolling around the village we commented on how beautiful it was, being full of flowers, cafes and lovely shoe shops. The church, which again dominated the village, sounded its bells at 12:00 noon and played the Ave Maria. How wonderful and peaceful it was here! We took lunch in the walled garden of a Brasserie; again it was wonderful, friendly and full of sunshine. After a meal of bœuf well done and salade, we made our way back to our baby. No one had touched her. The bags on the wheel arch racks were intact. The trunk rack bag was intact and our helmets, which Ned had secured with a plastic coated steel cable into a lock, were sitting there as we had left them.

Off we went on the D999 to the D32—Lacuane road. The terrain now was beautiful and took our breath away. The bends and drops were stupendous with mile after mile of hairpin bends. We were high up,

Just Us Two

one thousand five hundred metres at one point. Pine covered mountains and deep valleys went on and on for miles. It was totally unexpected and, on editing the camcorder film I found that it did not do it justice. Nothing can compare with the naked eye. Some roads had no reserve. If we went off the tarmac we would have been over the top. But—our baby did not let us down—she responded to every instruction, touch of the brakes and accelerator from her master.

From Lacaune we picked up the D907—the la Salvete and St Pons-de-Thomières road. St Pons was another lovely surprise. Again looking on the map, it was just another 'dot'. How wrong could we be? It was a delightful sleepy country village where we could have a rest and a drink in the local café attached to the hotel. The toilets were excellent. As is normal practice, I sent Ned on ahead to bring back a report. Having a nod of 'OK' I was pleasantly surprised to find how excellent they were with a button to turn around the sanitized seat covering. There I was, worrying if it would be a hole in the ground. Apart from Monte Carlo Casino, where the seat is rotated and cleaned, I had not seen this before. Our country is the one behind at times.

We continued on the D907 through vineyards. Many years ago, as a Retail Manager in the Wines and Spirits Trade, I had learnt about wines and their origin. Now I was seeing the country and vines, growing acre by acre, by the roadside. Big black juicy grapes hung in a bunch under the leaves of the vine. The vines were not tall—not like the vine tree of my youth which grew tall to the roof of the middle greenhouse on my father's land, before spreading its branches, full of big juicy black grapes, along the supports and the full length of the roof. These are small hardy bushes, no more than four feet high. Shielded from the fierce 'breeze' by trees, they were planted in rows where they marched along as they covered the land. This was Minervois land in the L'Aude valley. The scenery here was just as spectacular as the rest of the day had been with mile after mile of undulating land. It was so very green. I eventually espied a petrol station for a fill up as Ned's baby was thirsty. We continued to the D5 and D610 through the delightful village of Trèbes, riding alongside the Canal du Midi and the River Aude, over the flower-decked bridge to the N113 to Carcassonne via La Cité to our hotel. We intended to re-visit La Cité on the morrow and explore.

The morrow was to be a quiet day—or so we thought at first. We had a bit of indecision as to the mode of transport into town. We slowly began walking to find the launderette on the Square Gambetta in the centre. The sun was hot, so we turned back, collected the laundry and rode into Carcassonne centre. Last time we were here we stayed at the Ibis Hotel in the Square Gambetta. Although our present hotel was further out than expected, it was lovely with a nice reception, lounge area and excellent restaurant. Being out of town, parking facilities were ample. Overall, we had made a good choice as we found that the builders had taken over the huge Square Gambetta and much of the area in front of the Ibis Hotel. The launderette was right beside the Ibis Hotel and after parking off the other side of the square, using Ned's Blue Badge as it was too far to walk from the far end, we negotiated the intricacies of the French system of paying for powder and starting the machine. The Madame in charge was very helpful and with signs and demonstration explained that:

'All cash goes into one machine. You input the number of the machine be it Powder (which comes out of separate machine), Washing or Tumble Dryer. The machine starts automatically.'

With all this negotiated successfully, we were in business. *The biggest hurdle was the fierce looking black dog tied up outside the door.* Arriving back at the hotel, wearing only helmets for protective clothing, I remarked that this was what biking was all about. Just jump on and go and, as you can on a trike. As it was nearing lunchtime we bought postcards and settled down. We then decided that we did not want a big lunch and walked to the supermarket at the back. I enjoyed myself shopping French style as we chose provisions for a snack lunch. We set off in the even hotter sun to stroll gently, with many pauses for a rest, into La Cité! (I negotiated for a taxi ride back!). We had a lovely time exploring with Ned shooting pictures on his new camera of things that interested him, which includes: how buildings are built, gargoyles, brick construction, and the history of the place etc. etc., while I filmed what interested me like shops and pretty little courtyards, people bustling around and horse drawn wagons.

The horses looked very pretty with the lace caps on their ears to keep out the sun. We had a passer-by take one of us both and Ned took lots of the various parts of the medieval city.

An unforeseen circumstance.

Disaster now overtook us. The Ibis Central Hotel in Square Gambetta had helpfully arranged a taxi for us when we explained where we were staying. As we arrived back at our hotel, after a lovely afternoon and a bit of shopping, Ned was scrolling through his new camera to check battery life and space left etc on the SD card when, horror of horrors, he inadvertently clicked 'OK' for re-format and wiped out all our pictures! Ned was inconsolable, desolate even. I reminded him that it wasn't life and death, it was just for us.

'But I wanted pictures of Millau,' Ned said.

'Don't worry,' I said, 'I can do a 'grab frame' from the camcorder in the editing software, but first we need to check what I actually shot as I was using two hands to film'.

I had also wanted that last shot of La Cité to start the film with.

'We can go back in tomorrow before going to Trèbes and take some more shots of the city and perhaps you with the bike and the panorama of the city in the background'. I consoled him.

At the time of writing this we were playing back the videotape as I assured Ned that it could not be wiped off, if it ran to the end. I reflected that one solution was to have a laptop, the likes of which the young man who checked in earlier had. It was very slim and built into a zipped case which looked like a conference folder and I was quite taken with it. Then we could download the photos and have a back up. Always the best way—to have a contingency plan! We agreed that on the morrow we would ride back in and take some shots. Ned said that I had some good shots of the bridge which, considering I was taking photos at the same time and keeping my seat, was either a miracle or just good management and expertise!

As it happened, the following morning, Friday, Ned decided that we would not go back and take film of La Cité. We would use the camcorder film and 'grab frames'. Therefore, on our return home after I had loaded the film into my Studio Plus software on the computer and made a short film of the Viaduct for the men, I spent a whole day 'grabbing' frames from camcorder film so that I could add them to the DVD with the film. Due to the motion of the trike I lost some clarity but was able to fix some of it in my Adobe Photoshop software.

We strolled out to look at the Centro Commercial behind the hotel and looked into the clothes and shoe supermarkets. Ned & I were both looking at the same shoe (for him). It was a smart two-tone brown with trainer style soles and shoe style top and Velcro fastenings. He bought a pair. The children will be impressed with his choice as he is not noted for either shopping or being trendy.

We then togged up in helmets and gloves and took the back road to Trèbes. What a wonderful spot. We parked by the Canal du Midi and after getting a map at the Tourist Information Office on the canal bank we strolled through a tunnel of trees—which made a cooling walk—to the three locks, stopping along the way to take photos and watch the world go by. This was a ten minute walk which, in the event took us three hours. After taking photos of the staircase locks we went across to the other side for a lovely, leisurely set three-course lunch. It was 12:00 noon and time to eat French style. During lunch I stepped out to film a cruiser going through the locks. After strolling the few yards to where we had parked the bike we sat by the water's edge watching a lone swan gliding on the water, dipping its head to take a drink, and returning cruisers mooring up. Feeling sleepy we headed back for a siesta. We had planned the morrow's journey to Lourdes and were happy with the route but we began to have doubts about a long ride-out on Sunday as, even if we found a petrol station, petrol stations may not be open on a Sunday. Therefore, going over the border in the Pyrénées into Spain may not be a realistic or safe plan. (Don't forget, we had not brought the mobile phone.)

Carcassonne to Lourdes.

We set off early before the sun was up and headed south to Foix, following the N113 out of Carcassonne to the A61 and D4 before joining the D119 at Fanjeaux. At Vernoble we joined the D12 which took us to the N10 at Foix. As Foix came nearer we saw tantalising glimpses of the Haut Pyrénées towards Spain. We also passed a group of bikers one of which was a Gold Winger and saluted all. The signs for Andorre la Vella caused us to reflect on the last time we had travelled on this road in 2000 to the Andorra Drop Out ...

Turning westwards, we headed to St.Girons on the D117 to join the A64 at St.Gaudens to Tarbés and Lourdes. (Lourdes, apart from

Just Us Two

religious connections is a very pretty French town and a ski centre with trains going to about ten ski resorts.) Following the Ibis Hotel signs, we soon checked in and Ned put his very tired baby to bed in the secure allocated parking bay. We also were very tired and again debated on the wisdom of a journey out the following day. With a half a tank of petrol and no assurance of an open petrol station, in addition to a long journey to La Rochelle on the Monday, we decided against. During the afternoon we jostled our way through the streets full of bustling crowds speaking many languages and entered the peace and seclusion of the Domaine to visit La Grotte, sit quietly, reflect and absorb the peace which surrounded us to soothe our inner selves. (This private and personal part of our journey is not to be shared in too much detail.)

The following morning we made our way to the Domaine and sat by the open-air altar on the Esplanade. The Dublin contingent joined us and the priest romped through Mass in typical Irish fashion. The sermon was down to earth and thought provoking, talking about 'sayings' and 'actual meanings' and about crossroads and taking paths. We strolled around to the Grotto and lit a candle for the family. It was very peaceful with sounds of Masses and singing and church bells mingling together. On the way out, a little old nun whizzed past us on her mobility scooter at the rate of knots, terrifyingly fast, veil streaming behind her. She was in a hurry and no one was to get in her way. She was on a mission! After lunch and a rest we decided after all to have a little run out to Argelès-Gazot, Pierrefitte-Nestalas and down to Luz St.Sauveur. On our earlier, organised visits in '86, '88 and '91 there used to be a coach trip into the mountains and we had visited these places before, also Gavarnie and the Cirque de Gavarnie, Pont Napoleon, Cauterets and Pont D'Espagne. We thought it would have been good to visit some of these places again.

On our way out of Lourdes, playing our game of 'spot the petrol station,' I espied a Total garage on the left. It was open, so with a full tank we could go where we had wanted to without a worry. Taking the N21 we headed to Luz St. Saveur, joining the D921 at Pierfitte-Nestalas. French roads are good and we had no qualms about 'minor roads'. The scenery was out of this world and awe-inspiring. It was majestic with pine-covered mountains soaring high towards heaven; babbling streams—soon to be rivers—gathering the waters flowing down the mountainside and mountain villages slumbering quietly on this day of rest. The sun was high in the sky and those majestic pine covered mountains made a dramatic contrast to the clear blue sky.

Ned kept saying:

'I hope you are filming this view,' and 'I hope you are getting this footage.'

I was. My new summer gloves with air vents, soft leather, knuckle protectors (surrounded by lilac leather) and padded 'finger nails' were the perfect style for camcorder use as the hand strap fitted just so, as I pushed 'record' and 'pause'. This left only my left hand free to grab for safety as our motorised horse flew around the switchback roads in the brilliant sunshine. What fun! At Pont Napoleon there was a brisk business going on in bungee jumping and we stopped for photos of the gorge and ice cream. (This is obligatory on North Wales Wings ride-outs!)

At Gavarnie, we gazed again in awe at the Cirque de Gavarnie which is about eleven thousand feet high and visited the little church which, in days gone by, was the last stop of the pilgrims on their way to Santiago de Compestela in North West Spain, before going over the border. There are skulls of some of those who died on the way. After sitting in the shade under the trees Ned said that he wanted to go further up the road where we had parked, to see what there was as it appeared to be just a car park. This was an unmarked road, not visible on larger maps and would take us up to the Spanish Border. We would go through the passes of the Pic du Tentes approximately two thousand three hundred and thirty two metres. What an experience! We climbed higher and higher passing mobile homes; no tents here! This is camping French style and very civilised it is too with great provision made for their parking needs.

We met sheep, not only on the road but also on the switch back bends. Cows, (who knew their place) gazed at us silently as only cows can as they straddled the road on the bends. Higher and higher we went with Ned commenting with satisfaction that 'this was what the bike was made for' and he had been determined to take this ride. We found a flat turning area with the most stupendous views across the valleys and mountain ranges, from what appeared to us to be almost the top of the world. The mountain sheep were busy ringing their bells as they made their way slowly homewards in formation. Ned explained to me, that it was just the rams that had bells around their necks; that they kept their own ladies with them—just like in a harem. As it was by now getting late, we did not venture to the end of the road but, after photo shoots, made our way back. Ned was keen that I got all the shots of the road below. This was a fantastic sight, like ribbons of lace among the green fabric of the mountains. He said that he would go as close to the edge as he could so that I could capture the view, road patterns and gear changes. As it was a case of 'point and shoot and hang on', I did the best I could!

The mountains, as they appear in the distance are grey with a sharp outline and are majestic in the sky. As you draw nearer, they take on a different clothing of pine trees and appear friendlier. The return journey was the same. The mountains in the setting sun were like big humps—we see these in Wales on the return from Anglesey. We have always said that you go a long way to match North Wales. Today we did, in abundance.

As it was so hot the days seemed to be about two hours longer than we were used to. We had togged ourselves up in helmets and jeans and I wore sensible shoes, sacrificing my preferred footwear of mules. The cows were still munching by the side of the road as we came down the mountain. If we had been on two wheels I would have been very frightened as the cows lumbered slowly out of the way. Indeed some of the bends and cambers themselves would have been scary let alone meeting cows. On three wheels it was a different ball game and it has to be said that, other considerations apart, age is creeping up and I have had an extremely comfortable ride on our re-generated 'baby' and have the confidence of the extra wheel. For his part, Ned has found the EZ-Steer wonderful. It has been a long haul over the last three years but today our baby got its running shoes. Tomorrow would take us north to Bordeaux and La Rochelle for three nights. It was to be an unavoidable long ride for us now, so an early night was called for.

On the move again—To La Rochelle.
After an early start we made good time from Tarbes along the 'N' roads and 'A' roads north to La Rochelle. Long, long straight roads stretched into the distance as we travelled north. At Bordeaux we crossed the

River Garonne and then the River Dordogne as they flowed into the sea. In this region are acres and acres (or hectares) of vines with bunches of heavy black grapes. I still feel amazed at the size—or not—of the vines. *As narrated earlier, the vine my father had in the long middle greenhouse—where I grew up—rose to the roof and along its length. The sweetness of his heavy, plump and juicy bunches of grapes were famous to those in the know and callers to purchase were never in short supply.*

Arriving in La Rochelle, we followed the maps from the Internet together with the hotel's directions and found that we were staying very close to the old Vieux Port. We paid the four hours maximum at any one-time car-parking fee in the square opposite the hotel and, as it was now 3:10pm and there was no charge after 7:00pm, this took us to 9:10am the following morning. Strolling along the Quai Valin we drank in the lovely setting as boats bobbed on the water at their moorings and enthused that we had two full days to explore.

We had a quiet day in the town the following day. We strolled to the Tour St.Nicholas which was one of two tours or towers guarding the entrance to the harbour. The newer, larger quai had many, many boats and very large boatyards. It appeared to be a major industry here. We both found these interesting and had a lovely morning. Asking at the Tourist Information Office on the way back, we found that the Laverie Automatique (Launderette) was not far from our hotel. After a sandwich in a café near the hotel we dropped our camera back in our room at the hotel and went to do a reccae of the laundry ready for the morrow. Voila! There were four translations and it was similar to the one in Carcassonne with a central Paying Station. We strolled through the Vielle Ville area which is the medieval part of the town. From the laundry we crossed the footbridge over the canal and strolling past the church we happened upon a shop selling crafted sculptures and other Objects d' Art. As the shops close 12:00 noon–2:00pm for lunch we contented ourselves with window-shopping. There were some very unusual sculptures of people and birds etc. fusing coloured glass with bronze. This combined Ned's love of metal and my love of coloured glass. Unspoken, as we do, we both knew we were thinking the same thing. The moulded plaster pedestal in our sitting room was still awaiting a fitting sculpture (after fourteen years of waiting—again we haven't rushed things).

Just Us Two

We continued exploring and came upon Maison Henri II which is now the Town Hall. A must see visit for the morrow. The ornate stone arches and covered walkways in the street reminded us of the Chester Rows at home. As we strolled back, we reflected that we just had time to pop in and buy that sculpture before we had to feed the parking meter again at 3:11pm. After holding a sculpture of two birds up to the light to better see the glass and then the heron or stork (it is left to the imagination) we settled on the latter. It is 'quirky' with an expression as if to say *what* have they put on my head?' She is a one-off sculpture named Aigrette and we both fell for her. Satisfied that we had a fitting memento of our trip and a suitable finishing touch to our recent decorations, we strolled back and fed the meter bang on 3:11pm.

We spent Wednesday quietly by doing laundry. Ned insisted that we get there early as Wednesday morning was Happy Hour and he thought it would be busy. We arrived before 9:15am with our bag on my little trolley and he was wrong! It was quiet. Knowing the ropes by now, we fed the coin machine and sat watching the washing going round and round. Well—for a time as Ned soon found an interest in the table full of magazines, while I wandered outside to watch the town wake up. Later we quietly strolled around the medieval part of town and the other side of Quai Valin. It was lovely sitting in the sun under the trees and after finding a sandwich bar, returned to the seats for a leisurely lunch. Strolling through the medieval part of town we made a beeline for Maison Henri II. This edifice is a wonderful building on one side of a large square. We did not go into the house but contented ourselves with taking shots of the various parts of the courtyard. The streets around housed old buildings e.g. Corn Exchange, which have arched, covered walkways which shields the walker from the sun as they browse the smart shops within.

Feeling tired, we strolled back to our hotel for a rest where a hive of activity greeted us; lots of Plasma TV's were being prepared for installation. The manager said that they would do ours in ten minutes. (That was on his time clock anyway.) We de-camped to the courtyard for a quiet drink and relaxed in the sun. It was then time to pack up again and plan the route for our journey to Bretagne on the homeward stretch.

To Bretagne.

We had intended an early start at 6.00am on the Thursday but there was no need for an alarm as, long before this, we heard a lot of shouting and banging.

'What on earth …?' 'There is no need for that …!' Ned shouted as he jumped awake.

'Perhaps it is the late home comers from the clubs …' I murmured sleepily.

At 6:00am Ned went to the bathroom to start the day and remembered the hotel notice in our room about fines for parking in front of the hotel on Thursdays.

'Ohhhhh! It is Thursday!' He exclaimed in panic.

Donning trousers, he grabbed his keys and dashed out. Returning he was incredulous at what he had seen.

'The police are there and they are just strapping up cars and lifting them onto a low-loader and towing them away!' Ned exclaimed in disbelief.

'Is the bike OK?' I asked.

'Yes, yes, I have moved it up by the pavement outside the hotel entrance,' Ned answered.

We realised that it must be a Market Day. I was on tenterhooks until we were able to set off, as we had loaded the bags in dribs and drabs ready for a quick getaway and I was worried that they might take away the bike and the bags with it. We had kept an eagle eye on our baby as we had breakfast, although it did appear that where we had parked would not have been a problem. But—I mean—to just tow away—and what about business people who had parked last night and had appointments today? We were grateful for the advance notices from the hotel but as there were no notices around the car park, it was a bit *off*! In any case, only fines were mentioned—not removal.

However, our baby was safe and we set off from La Rochelle to Bretagne and Bréhan which is between Pontivy and Josselin. First though we had to play 'spot the petrol station' and found it as marked on our map by the hotel receptionist (I had marked one on our Internet map which showed it to be by the hotel but this turned out to be an electrical re-charging point, possibly for electric cars.) The journey north was uneventful, taking us north towards Nantes along the Autoroute, N165 west to Vannes and D767/D17 and D2 to our destination. I dozed along the way and we detoured off the main road by the Gulf Morhiban to lunch on our sandwiches. The little village with a bridge over the water was delightful and we watched the duck on one side which wanted our lunch and the seagulls on the sandbanks on the other side. They flew lazily around in the sunshine and two herons lined up to make a graceful take-off into the sky. Oh! To be a bird without a care in the world! What a life! A Gold Wing roared up and parked by the café. It was 12:00 noon and time for the French workers to have lunch.

Nearing our destination, again we needed petrol and knew, from our last visit, that there was one in Rohan, only a couple of miles from Bréhan. Ned rang the bell for the attendant and started to unhook the pump. The attendant strolled out of his car repair shop and 'smacked his hand' so to speak for doing self-service.

'*I do!*' he said sternly.

What struck Ned was that as he came out of his repair shop he picked up his hat to wear against the sun. Obviously he wasn't going to rush.

'A completely different way of life,' he said.

As Ned had forgotten the mobile (yes, I keep reminding him of that as he calls himself Mr Perfect!) and I had handed mine in to College when I retired two weeks previously, we had phoned ahead from the hotel to make meeting arrangements which went as planned and we spent the next day and half, relaxing. In the evening we rode into the village to the supermarket and an old man (older than us), rode past on his bicycle and nearly fell off as he saw our beautiful baby. Apart from family reunions, we were glad to see Maguire who is the softest dog you could imagine—an Irish wolfhound, who I swear, understands everything. In addition we found that the self-adopted stray cat had had kittens in the attic of the old animal shelter. The following morning we took a gentle stroll down the country lanes around Bréhan. This is a country village and very sleepy, yet …, there seemed to be a lot of cars around with smartly dressed people going into church. There was a classic car parked outside which was decked out in tulle bows and flowers (Ned said that this had been driven from the florists the previous evening and the driver had had a huge smile on his face). We peeped into the church and heard the strains of:

'You'll never walk alone,' in English? We could hardly believe our ears.

'Is it to do with the rugby as there are banners outside the village bar?' we wondered as it was quite a big thing in France. I opened the door and heard:

'He guided us in times of trouble.'

'Perhaps it is a funeral, but the church is packed and there are flowers in the car,' we said.

A mystery! On our way back many tractors passed us in the lane. It was nearly 12:00 noon and lunchtime (In France, midday meal is an important occasion. From 12:00 noon–2.00pm everywhere closes down while everyone has a good lunch—with wine etc.—before going back to work). Arriving back at my brother's home we related all that had happened and he thought it strange too. We set off to go to the local restaurant for lunch. I made sure that we had a good table by the window opposite the church as I wanted a solution to the mystery and we were all intrigued. The four course lunch with a choice of wine, cider, water—or all three and re-fill the wine carafe from the barrel if needed— plus coffee, was delicious and all for €10.50cents. We all decided that the cheese course would be too much though and kept a watchful eye on the church. As we ate, a van—painted pink and decorated as a pig, together with waving ears with names on them—pulled up. It was a wedding!

Homeward bound via Caen and Dunkerque.

We left sleepy Bréhan early on Saturday morning saying good-bye to my brother, Maguire the dog and the stray cat & its kittens. We were booked into the Ibis Caen on the Periphique which we thought would be easy to find. We had vaguely planned to visit Bayeux nearby but, realistically it was not an option after travelling one hundred and eighty miles. The day had been misty as we left Bretagne and turned damp and cold as we travelled through Le Manche and were happy to relax and have a lovely meal in the restaurant. We fervently hoped that the chills of today would not repeat themselves on the morrow.

Just Us Two

Sunday dawned and, as we had to catch the 4:00pm ferry we needed an early start to cover two hundred miles. Ned estimates an average of 50mph on the trike due to petrol consumption but, in truth, I often saw the needle at 65mph and more which is good going for a trike.

It was a crisp morning as we set off from Caen at 7:30am. Riding round the Periphique, the rising sun was on our left, right, then straight ahead as we followed the signs to take us northwards (signposted Paris at this point). The sun was a huge red ball in the sky and, as it rose, spread its beams like fingers through the clouds to touch and warm all around. A magnificent sunrise! As we rode on, the crisp early morning turned to a quite chilly one. We did not realise that we had climbed quite so high. We stopped before Honfleur to stretch our legs and, armed now with the camcorder, I was ready to film once again the Pont du Normandie. This is an impressive sight as it crosses from Le Havre to Honfleur and quite as impressive as the Millau Viaduct. There are actually two bridges here of different designs. The sun rose now in the sky and the landscape changed to a more scenic and hilly variety. I was able to catch, on the camcorder, our shadows on the road from the rising sun which shows 'just us two' battling it out together. We had lunch near Boulogne and a group of pensioners on a coach trip sent us on our way with a 'thumbs up' sign. We had their approval! Laughing, I returned with 'two thumbs up' as we headed off for the last few miles to Dunkerque and our ferry to Dover, family in the South West of England and then the wonderful hills of North Wales and home. (On the ferry, we settled ourselves just in time for Ned to watch the motor racing on the wide screen TV which was, for him, the perfect end to our trip. As we made our way back to the car deck, we paused outside to look at the looming land. Oh, look Ned, there is our trike! Ned was not a happy bunny as he realised that where we had been directed (behind bikes even though we had booked on as a car) was out in the open. He was fuming to think of all the salty sea spray which must be giving his baby a shower. He calmed down a little when he reflected that it not much different than riding along the promenade at Blackpool where the sea spray crashes in over the railings).

On entering the restaurant at our hotel in Dover, we were brought back to earth from our happy holiday memories to be greeted by the sight in the foyer of a *fully dressed Christmas tree.*

'In the middle of September?' we wondered, amazed.

Final thoughts.

All in all this, probably last, 'long' journey of the Way Worn Winger and his 'chick' has taken two thousand six hundred and fifteen miles, eighteen days, ten hotels and numerous unforgettable sights and experiences. The last long journey that is, until one day I pick up the maps and say:

'What about going to…?'

Or Ned says in his usual fashion:

'Howzabout …?'

We shall see …

Ned & Rosie x x

Cirque du Gavarnie high in the Pyrenees
Near the Spanish Border

Just Us Two -
Gavarnie les Especieres in the Pyrenees
near the Spanish Border

Epilogue

Never say 'Never'

So there you are you empty nesters. Life is not over when you start to feel a mid-life crisis descend upon you. Live for today, spend the children's inheritance, buy a bike preferably a Gold Wing—and explore.

In over ten years we have travelled over 50,000 miles for pure pleasure in what has been a life-changing experience, had a lot of fun, met new challenges and have 'grown and stretched' within ourselves as we have travelled on Ned's baby. This baby of mine has been incubating for ten years and is now ready to be 'born' in order that you too can share in our discoveries and adventures. I hope that you have had a pleasant journey.

The underlying message of this tale is to take what life offers, do what you can while you can and, overall to trust in God. Draw strength to overcome obstacles and with hope, focus on what is possible.

Later, much, much later I heard a voice saying:

'Rosie, next year I want six weeks in Italy,' as the pleading sound of Ned's voice, came across my Birthday dinner table early the following year.

'I want to do the leg of Italy …,' he said.

'In that case I will have to finish my book!' I replied.

'And I want to hire a Boom Trike when we go to Fuerteventura next month …' he pleaded. (We did.)

Sadly, however, after buying maps of Italy, Austria, Germany, and Switzerland in the summer of 2008 and making plans, we realised that Italy was a step too far for us now on the bike. Then, during a touring holiday in the UK later in 2008, we reluctantly realised that we would have to hang up our riding boots, sell our beloved Gold Wing and revert to four wheels.

'Since we have done what you wanted to for ten years, can we do what I want to now?' Rosie asked.

'What is that' Ned asked warily.

'When we sell the Gold Wing, we should trade in the car and buy that open-topped tourer I have longed for, for years. We can still tour. You have got used to the roads abroad.'

'OK', agreed Ned promptly.

Rosie had the last word of course:

'I want my share of the driving Ned ...'

Silence.

Never say 'Never'!

THE END

Printed in the United Kingdom by
Lightning Source UK Ltd., Milton Keynes
141132UK00002B/9/P